CHINESE COOKERY

GAIL DUFF

HAMLYN

Produced by New Leaf Productions

Photography by Mick Duff
Design by Jim Wire
Series Editor: Sarah Wallace

First published in 1984 by Hamlyn Publishing
Bridge House, London Road,
Twickenham, Middlesex, England

© Copyright Hamlyn Publishing 1984, a division of
The Hamlyn Publishing Group Limited

Third impression 1985

ISBN 0 600 20807 9

Printed in Spain

Larsa D. L. TF. 931 – 1984

NOTE

1. Metric and imperial measurements have been
calculated separately. Use one set of measurements only
as they are not exact equivalents.

2. All spoon measures are level unless otherwise stated.

3. All recipes serve 4 unless otherwise stated.

CONTENTS

INTRODUCTION

Chinese food has become extremely popular in the West in recent years. Chinese restaurants or take-away food shops can be found in almost any town and for many families at least one Chinese meal a week has become accepted practice.

Once a style of cuisine has been accepted, it does not take too long before adventurous cooks want to try their hand at it themselves. At first they may have to adapt their own equipment and ingredients to produce dishes as near as possible to the original, but as more and more people decide that they would like to produce these once-foreign dishes in their own kitchens, kitchenware shops, specialist food shops and finally the supermarkets make both equipment and ingredients more readily available.

This is exactly what has happened with Chinese food. You may find specialist Chinese shops in many large towns. The herbs, spices and sauces needed to prepare authentic dishes can be bought in wholefood shops and delicatessens, and the range of Chinese ingredients to be found in supermarkets is on the increase. As for equipment, you cannot enter a kitchenware shop without finding at least 2 types of wok together with their stands, utensils and sets of chopsticks.

The Chinese style of cooking is vastly different from that found in the West, but this does not mean to say that it is difficult.

In fact, once the basic techniques have been mastered, you will find that it is incredibly easy. Combine these techniques with the wealth of fresh ingredients that are available to the Chinese cook and you will discover a whole new world of colourful and exciting recipes.

The regions of China

China can be roughly divided into 4 main regions, each one with a different style of cooking.

The northern region includes the city of Peking and the areas of Shantung, Honan and Hopei. Peking was once the home of the Emperor of China and he naturally attracted the best chefs in the country to his court, each one seeking to outdo his predecessor in inventiveness and presentation. This brought a certain elegance of style to the area.

Peking cooking has also been influenced by the invasions of the Tartars and Mongols who brought with them Moslem traditions, including a liking for mutton and lamb not found elsewhere in China. In fact Peking has often been referred to as the 'Mutton City of China'.

Roasting, barbequeing and boiling are favourite cooking methods of the region and the final dishes are rather drier than those from other areas.

The staple food of the North is wheat rather than rice and so noodles, steamed breads and buns, and pancakes are popular.

Large prawns from the sea are cooked in their shells. Crabs come from the Yellow River and so too does carp which is cooked to produce a sweet and sour dish.

Many vegetables are grown in the northern region, the favourite being Chinese cabbage. Garlic, onions, shallots and leeks are used extensively; so too is fresh ginger root. Sesame oil, seeds and paste – legacies from the Tartars – are also popular.

The most famous dish of the region is Peking duck with its crispy skin served separately and its accompaniments of savoury dips and Mandarin pancakes.

The coastal or eastern region of China includes the city of Shanghai and the areas of Fukien, Anwei, Kiangse and Kiangsu. The Yangtze River flows through the region and Shanghai is situated on a delta where the land is more fertile than any in China. Here are grown both wheat and rice, barley, corn, sweet potatoes, soya beans and vegetables.

Fish and shellfish naturally feature a great deal in the cooking of the region and these are usually very gently spiced and cooked to bring out their fresh flavours. Phoenix tailed prawns and deep-fried prawn balls are favourite foods around the Yangtze Delta.

Kiangse is known as the 'Land of Fish and Rice'. A speciality is meat balls steamed in a coating of rice; and the noodles here are made from rice rather than wheat.

Fukien produces what some consider to be the best soy sauce in China and so there is a good deal of what is known as red-cooking – simmering meats with soy sauce and spices. Around Shanghai the soy sauce is used to produce sweet, salty dishes with plenty of sauce.

In Kiangsu and Anwei, pork and poultry are widely used. You will find dishes such as Lions' Heads (a casserole of pork balls), red-cooked pork with eggs and salted chicken.

The western region of China is composed of the areas of Szechuan and Yunnan. It has no sea coast, but the Yangtze River flows through on its way to the sea and freshwater fish are plentiful.

More cattle are kept in Szechuan than in any other region and therefore there is a predominance of beef dishes. Cheaper cuts such as shin are stewed slowly in lightly flavoured broth and the fore cuts such as rump and fillet are what is known as dry-fried – that is, stir-fried with no liquid and with only a small amount of sauce added to the final dish.

Salting, drying, pickling and smoking are all favourite food preparations in the western region. The speciality of Yunnan is a cured and smoked ham which is served raw. Hot and sour vegetable pickles come from Szechuan. Chicken, duck and fish are often steamed with salt and Szechuan pepper and then smoked briefly over burning sugar.

Seven flavours make up the cuisine of the western region. There is sweetness from honey and sugar; saltiness from soy sauce and salt; sourness from vinegar and pickles; bitterness from spring onions and leeks; fragrance from fresh ginger root and garlic; a nutty quality from sesame paste and oil; and a hotness from chillis, hot pepper oil and Szechuan pepper. These are often combined to make sauces to pour over cooked dishes both hot and cold and to make pastes to add to dry-fried dishes. Specialities of the area include smoked chicken, noodles with sesame sauce, pork with transparent noodles and coin-purse eggs.

The southern region is made up of the area around the city of Canton, including the areas of Kwangsi and Kwangtung. Cantonese cooking has become the most familiar in the West since the first Chinese restaurants were opened by emigrants from Canton itself and from the neighbouring British protectorate of Hong Kong.

There is another reason why Cantonese food has been so celebrated. In 1644 the Ming dynasty, then centred in Peking, was overthrown and the Imperial household fled to Canton. The chefs collected recipes on their way South and combined their native Peking style of cooking with that of Canton. As a result, the cooking of Canton became the most original, varied and best presented in the whole of China.

Vegetables are abundant in the South, either stir-fried alone or with meats. Fruit is often used in meat and poultry dishes to give a sweet and sour effect. Another unusual combination is that of meat and seafood. In some dishes they are cooked together and in others an oyster or lobster sauce is used to flavour meats.

There is a distinct light savouriness to Cantonese food. Ginger is used extensively and the natural flavours of the basic ingredients are brought out by steaming, stir-frying and roasting. The soy sauce used here is a lighter type than that used in other areas but a highly savoury quality is given to some dishes by the addition of a salty black bean paste or hoisin sauce.

Typical Cantonese dishes include sweet and sour pork, beef in oyster sauce, velvet chicken and corn soup and Cha Shao (marinated and quickly roasted pork). A speciality of the area not found elsewhere are the steamed buns known as dim sum.

INGREDIENTS AND COOKING TECHNIQUES

Sauces

Soy sauce This is a rich tasting, slightly salty sauce of a thin consistency that is made from soya beans. It can be bought in supermarkets, delicatessens and wholefood shops. In specialist Chinese shops you will find 2 types, a dark one and a lighter one. The dark one is most often used in cooking. The lighter one is used for more delicately flavoured dishes and is also served as a condiment at the table.

A mushroom-flavoured soy sauce can be used to give added flavour to dishes, especially those containing mushrooms.

Hoisin sauce Hoisin sauce is also made from soya beans. A thick, brown sauce with a hot, slightly sweet flavour, it is used to flavour some stir-fried dishes and as a dip for plainly cooked meats. It can be bought in Chinese shops and delicatessens.

Chilli sauce Chilli sauce is made from red chillis. A red-orange colour and very hot, it is about the same consistency as tomato ketchup and may or may not be flavoured with garlic. It can be bought in Chinese and other specialist food shops.

Oyster sauce Oyster sauce is made from oysters and soy beans. Thick and salty and often used to flavour beef dishes, once opened it should be kept in the refrigerator. It can be bought in Chinese and other specialist food shops.

Plum sauce Plum sauce is thick and fruity and is usually only available from Chinese shops.

Bean pastes These are also referred to as bean sauces and are made from soya beans. They were once available only from Chinese food shops but they are becoming easier to buy in the West. Once opened, bean pastes should be stored in the refrigerator.

Yellow bean paste This is sometimes called brown bean paste. Thick and yellow-brown and with a rich, slightly sweet flavour, it is used to make thick sauces and dressings, dips and some marinades.

Black bean paste Slightly less thick than the yellow paste, black bean paste is dark brown to black in colour and has a lighter, salty, hot flavour. It is used in stir-fried dishes and in dips.

Spices

Star anise Star anise comes in the form of a dried, star-shaped seed pod that is usually added to braised and simmered dishes to give a slight liquorice flavour. It can be bought from specialist herb and spice shops and also from Chinese shops.

Five-spice powder This is a mixture of 5 ground spices – aniseed, Szechuan pepper, fennel seed, cloves and cinnamon. It can be bought from delicatessens, some wholefood shops and from Chinese shops.

Szechuan pepper Szechuan peppercorns are red-brown in colour and have a stronger, more pungent flavour than black pepper. If they are unavailable, black peppercorns can be used instead.

Dried chillis Available from most shops that sell spices, dried chillis are used crushed in some sauces and also to flavour oil.

Herbs

Coriander Coriander comes from the same family as parsley and is sometimes called Chinese parsley. It has a slightly sweet, pungent flavour. Coriander can be bought fresh in Chinese shops and some markets and can also be grown as an annual in Western herb gardens. This is the only fresh herb used in Chinese cooking.

Vegetables

Ginger root Although used essentially for flavouring, ginger root is really a tuberous vegetable. It has a knobbly appearance, rather like a Jerusalem artichoke and a silvery, light brown skin. The texture is rather fibrous and if it is to be incorporated into a dish it is usually grated before being added to the rest of the ingredients. If ginger root is to be used for flavouring only, such as in a simmered meat dish, it is sliced and then removed before the dish is served.

Fresh ginger, as opposed to the ground variety, gives a light, almost citrus flavour to dishes and can be bought from Chinese food shops and some greengrocers.

Chillis Besides chilli sauce, fresh green and red chillis are used in some Chinese dishes, particularly in those from Szechuan. Chillis are related to green and red peppers, only they are smaller and have a very hot flavour. Before use they should be cored and seeded. Fresh chillis can be bought from Chinese and other ethnic shops and from some greengrocers.

Bean sprouts Fresh bean sprouts can now be bought in many supermarkets and greengrocers and they are always available in Chinese shops. You can also sprout your own, using dried mung beans. They are best used on the day of purchase but will keep for up to 2 days in a polythene bag in the refrigerator.

Bamboo shoots Readily available in tins from supermarkets, grocers and Chinese shops, bamboo shoots can be bought either sliced or in chunky pieces. They need only be drained before use.

Water chestnuts Water chestnuts are a small, round tuberous vegetable, white and crispy and with a fresh flavour. Like bamboo shoots, they are readily available in tins and need only be drained before use.

Chinese mushrooms These are a special variety of dried mushroom that is usually only available from Chinese shops. Chinese mushrooms must be soaked in boiling water for at least 20 minutes before use. They have a chewy texture and stronger flavour than cultivated mushrooms and only a few are needed for any dish.

Nuts and oils
Cashew nuts, almonds and peanuts These can be bought from most supermarkets and grocers.
Sesame seeds These are very small seeds with a slightly bitter, nutty flavour. They can be bought from wholefood shops, some supermarkets and from Chinese shops.
Sesame paste This can be bought from Chinese shops and from wholefood shops where it is also called tahini. It is a light grey paste made of pure ground sesame seeds.
Sesame oil This is a nutty flavoured oil extracted from sesame seeds. Sesame oil is used mainly to enrich and flavour dishes just before serving and also for dips and salad dressings.
Peanut oil Although most recipes in this book do not specify which type of oil to use, peanut oil is the one that is most favoured by the Chinese. It is also called groundnut oil and is readily available from supermarkets, grocers and wholefood shops.

Dried seafood
Dried seafood is used to give a highly flavoured salty quality to some dishes. Dried shrimps are the most common. Dried seafood is only available from Chinese shops.

Wines and Spirits
Rice wine Used to flavour many dishes, Chinese rice wine can be bought from some Chinese shops and is also stocked by a few wine merchants. A pale dry sherry makes an excellent substitute.
Kao Liang spirit This is a Chinese spirit made from sorghum and millet. If it is unobtainable, brandy can be used instead.

Chinese cooking techniques
Stir-frying This is the most popular Chinese cooking method in the West. The food is sliced into thin, uniform pieces and cooked very quickly on a high heat in a small amount of oil, while being moved around continuously in the pan. Meat and vegetables can be cooked separately or together using this method.
Stir-braising For this method, the food is first stir-fried and liquid and perhaps a cornflour thickener are added. The food is then covered and cooked on a slightly lower heat in the liquid.
Shallow-frying Larger pieces of food, usually fish or meat, are fried on a moderate heat in slightly more oil than is used for stir-frying and for a longer time.
Deep-frying The deep-frying process in Chinese cookery is exactly the same as that in the West but it is more imaginatively applied. For example, a whole duck or chicken can be deep-fried after an initial steaming process; or small pieces of meat can be deep-fried before being stir-fried with other ingredients.
Simmering Meat and fish can be simmered for a long time in a clear, lightly flavoured broth. Clear soups can also be cooked by this method. In China, an earthenware pot called a sandpot is stood over a low charcoal fire, but a heavy, flameproof casserole over a low flame is almost as effective. Simmered foods can be served in the broth. Meats and poultry can be served either plainly with dips after simmering or finished off by deep-frying.
White-cooking This is usually applied to white meats such as chicken and pork. They are cooked on top of the stove in water which has only spring onions and a little ginger root for flavour. The result is a pale coloured, moist meat which is often served with separate sauces or dips. Vegetables such as savoy cabbage or Chinese cabbage can also be white-cooked.
Red-cooking This technique is often used for whole joints of meat and for poultry. The meat is simmered in a large amount of soy sauce plus a little water and some rice wine or dry sherry. Sometimes sugar or ginger root are added. The result is not really red but a deep brown colour.
Steaming Fish is often rapidly steamed whole on an open dish inside a wok. Food which takes longer to steam such as beef with Chinese mushrooms (p. 38) is generally wrapped in lotus leaves or Chinese cabbage leaves. Bread, buns and cakes are also steamed.
Roasting Chinese food is often marinated before roasting to give it extra flavour. It can be quick-roasted at a high temperature or slow roasted, sometimes after having been simmered in a flavoured liquid.

EQUIPMENT AND ETIQUETTE

Special equipment

Chopping board Chinese chefs like to use a round wooden chopping board which is made by cutting a 10-cm/4-in section of a tree trunk. This is not essential but it is a very useful item in any kitchen. Chopping boards can be bought in Chinese shops.

Cleaver Instead of a set of cook's knives, a Chinese chef will probably own 2 meat cleavers – a heavy one for chopping meat on the bone and a lighter one which is used to thinly slice and finely chop both meats and vegetables. The broad blade of the cleaver is also often used to carry prepared foods from the chopping board to the pot. Meat cleavers can be bought in Chinese shops and from specialist kitchen shops.

Wok The wok has become almost as popular a utensil in the Western kitchen as it is in Chinese kitchens. Most woks are shaped like a wide cone with a rounded base and 2 handles. They were originally designed to be used over an open brazier so that heat could be evenly distributed around the base and sides. Some woks now sold in the West have a flattened base enabling them to be used on conventional stoves. Others come with a round stand that will keep the wok in place on either a gas or electric ring.

Woks are used for both stir-frying and deep-frying, for steaming, simmering and braising. Like the cleaver they are extremely versatile.

To make the best use of this versatility, make sure that your wok is fitted with a large, domed lid. Some woks have a stand that will fit inside to take a dish of steamed fish or a special steamer. Some have a rack that fits over the rim. This is often used when you are deep frying food in several batches. The portions already cooked can drain and keep warm on the rack while the others are cooking.

Fish slice The fish slice used in Chinese cookery is shaped rather like a shovel with a rounded blade. This makes it easier to use in the round-sided wok. It may be solid or have perforations.

Ladle A Chinese ladle is exactly the same shape as a Western one but slightly smaller.

Strainers Small, round strainers are useful for lifting fried food out of the wok.

Steamers Food can be steamed in a dish placed on a stand inside a wok. For food that is open steamed such as steamed buns or rice-coated meat balls, use a round bamboo steamer. This will fit well on the stand inside the wok and can be easily covered by the domed lid. The steamer very often has 2 or more tiers, thus allowing several types of food to be steamed simultaneously.

Using Western equipment

Although Chinese cookery equipment is relatively inexpensive you may still rather use your conventional equipment.

A good chopping board and a set of cook's knives are standard equipment in most kitchens. Instead of a wok, use a good-quality heavy frying pan, the larger the better. A frying pan with a diameter of 25cm/10in is ideal.

A large vegetable steamer can be used instead of a bamboo steamer.

Planning and serving a Chinese meal

There is very rarely just one main dish served at a Chinese meal. It is general practice in China to serve one main dish per person, so if there were 4 people there would be as many main dishes. There would also be one soup or a selection of appetizers and perhaps another very light, clear soup that was served during the meal.

For a family meal, all the main dishes and accompaniments such as rice or noodles are put on the table together and everyone helps themselves to

whatever they want. At a party or banquet with 6 or more people there may be up to 3 appetizers, two hot and one cold. The selection of main dishes will then be served one after the other, so that each person tries every dish.

Just one sweet is usually served to end a family meal. There would probably be a choice of two at a banquet, put on the table together.

When you are deciding on the dishes to serve at a Chinese meal, remember to make them as varied as possible. Choose a selection of different cooking methods and different types of basic ingredients (meat, poultry, fish, bean curd and so on). Make sure the dishes give you a wide variety of flavour and richness, texture and colour, size and shape.

Setting the table
Chinese food is eaten from bowls instead of plates.

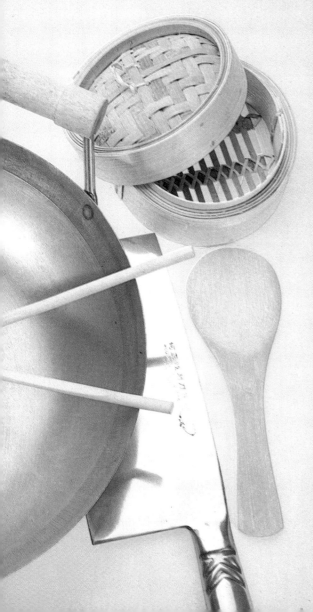

In China, just one bowl, one spoon and one set of chopsticks is given to each person. Soups are put into a large serving bowl in the middle of the table and each person drinks from it with his/her own spoon throughout the meal. You may find it more convenient to provide 2 bowls, one for the soup and one for the main meal. In this case a soup ladle should be provided.

Chopsticks are used for everything in China, even rice, which is scooped into the mouth from a raised bowl. They are used to take food from the serving dishes to your own bowls as well as for actually eating. If you know that your friends can use chopsticks easily, you can follow this pattern. If not, provide spoons as well. Of course, there is really no reason why you should not use plates and knives and forks. It depends on how authentic an atmosphere you wish to create.

What to drink with a Chinese meal
The Chinese do not drink alcohol before a meal. It is reserved for serving with the food. Before the food arrives, guests might well quench their thirsts with a refreshing cup of fragrant China tea. A stronger brew of tea is also drunk at the end of the meal.

China tea is light and fragrant and it should be enjoyed without milk or sugar. There are basically 2 types, green or unfermented tea and red or black tea which has been fermented to give a stronger flavour. Lapsang Souchong tea is a favourite in the West. It is a smoked black tea from Hunan. Teas flavoured with rose petals, jasmine flowers and lychees are also available. Keemum is a black tea from Anwei. Dragon Well and Lu An teas are both green teas. Oolong tea is semi-fermented and the most expensive.

Where most of the dishes in a meal are on the dry side it is often the custom to serve a very light, clear soup throughout the meal as a thirst quencher and also to clear the palate of the flavour of one dish before the next is served.

Chinese wine is often served throughout a meal. It is not made from grapes but from a special rice called glutinous rice. Rice wines are also called yellow wines and the most famous is Shiao Hsing.

Very strong spirit wines are also drunk with Chinese food. The most popular is called Mao Tai. Grape wines can also be served with Chinese food. Whichever you choose, it is the Chinese custom for the host to begin the drinking. He raises his glass to the guest of honour and says 'Kan Pei!'. The guests may then toast each other, downing the contents of the glass in one gulp and turning their glasses upside down on the table and repeating the same toast – 'Kan Pei!' – Bottoms Up!

APPETIZERS AND SOUPS

There are no specific appetizer dishes in Chinese cooking. Main dishes and cold meats are served in smaller portions, garnished perhaps with eggs or seafood. Serve one or two for a family meal or perhaps a whole platter with a choice of 6 or more items for a party.

The following dishes in the book can be used as appetizers:

Barbequed prawns, p. 16
Phoenix tailed prawns, p. 17
Cha Shao (roast pork), served cold and thinly
    sliced, p. 26
Pork kidney salad, p.31
Chinese stewed beef, served cold and thinly
    sliced, p. 35
Jellied lamb, served in small, thin slices, p. 42

Cantonese crystal chicken, p. 46
Deep-fried paper-wrapped chicken, p. 47
Tea eggs, p. 50.
Soy eggs, p. 50
Deep-fried pork wontons, p. 73
Pork and vegetable spring roll, p. 74
Pork and prawn egg roll, p. 75

Chinese soups are usually very light, seldom rich and creamy like those in Western cooking. Sweet-corn is a popular ingredient and beaten eggs are often poured into the soup in a thin stream so they set in strands.

The following soups are all suitable for serving at the beginning of the meal.

SWEETCORN AND EGG SOUP

100g/4 oz lean pork
1 tbsp cornflour
1 tsp ground ginger
1 tbsp oil
1 tbsp soy sauce
salt and freshly ground black pepper
900ml/1½ pints chicken stock
one 440-g/15-oz tin creamed sweetcorn
2 tbsp rice wine or dry sherry
2 eggs, beaten
2 spring onions, finely chopped

Mince or very finely chop the pork. Mix the pork with the cornflour, ginger, oil and soy sauce and season well.

Put the stock into a saucepan and bring to the boil. Put in the pork and simmer for 10 minutes. Add the sweetcorn and sherry and reheat the soup. When the soup is just below boiling point, add the eggs in a thin stream, pouring them over the prongs of a fork. Stir well.

Pour the soup into individual bowls and scatter the chopped spring onions over the top.

WATERCRESS SOUP

100g/4 oz watercress
900ml/1½ pints chicken stock
2 tbsp soy sauce
4 tbsp rice wine or dry sherry
1 tsp salt
freshly ground black pepper
2 eggs, beaten
4 spring onions, finely chopped
2 tsp sesame oil

Finely chop the watercress. Put the stock into a saucepan, bring to the boil and add the soy sauce, wine or sherry and seasonings.

Turn down the heat and let the soup come off the boil. Pour in the eggs in a thin stream, over the prongs of a fork. Add the watercress and bring the soup back to the boil.

Scatter in the spring onions and the sesame oil just before serving.

VELVET CHICKEN AND CORN SOUP

1 chicken breast
2 tbsp rice wine or dry sherry
¼ tsp salt
2 egg whites
900ml/1½ pints chicken stock
1 tbsp soy sauce
one 350-g/12-oz tin sweetcorn
1½ tbsp cornflour mixed with 3 tbsp cold water
50g/2 oz lean cooked ham, finely chopped

Mince the chicken breast and mix with the wine or sherry and salt. Add the egg whites and mix well.

Put the chicken stock into a saucepan and bring to the boil. Add the chicken and simmer for 5 minutes. Add the soy sauce and sweetcorn and stir in the cornflour and water. Bring the soup back to the boil and stir until it thickens.

Pour the soup into individual bowls and garnish with the chopped ham.

HOT AND SOUR SOUP

4 Chinese mushrooms
1 tbsp dried shrimps
100g/4 oz lean pork
½ tsp salt
2 tbsp cornflour
3 tbsp cold water
150g/5 oz bean curd
900ml/1½ pints stock
1 tbsp soy sauce
2 tbsp red wine vinegar
2 eggs, beaten
freshly ground black pepper
2 tsp sesame oil
2 tbsp chopped fresh coriander or parsley

Soak the mushrooms in boiling water for 20 minutes. Drain and cut into thin strips. Soak the shrimps in boiling water for 10 minutes. Drain and chop the shrimps. Cut the pork into small, thin strips. Mix with the salt and ½ tbsp cornflour. Mix the remaining cornflour with cold water. Cut the bean curd into thin strips the same size as the pork.

Put the stock into a saucepan and bring to the boil. Put in the pork and simmer for 5 minutes. Add the mushrooms, shrimps, bean curd, soy sauce and vinegar. Stir in the cornflour and water. Bring the soup gently back to the boil and stir until it thickens.

Pour in the eggs in a thin stream, over the prongs of a fork. Stir well and season with plenty of pepper.

Pour the soup into a large serving bowl or into individual bowls. Sprinkle the top with sesame oil and garnish with the coriander or parsley.

CUCUMBER SOUP

225g/8 oz lean pork
½ tbsp cornflour
1 tbsp rice wine or dry sherry
2 tbsp soy sauce
1 cucumber
900ml/1½ pints chicken stock
1 tbsp white wine vinegar
½ tsp salt

Cut the pork into small, thin slices and mix with the cornflour, sherry and 1 tbsp soy sauce. Peel and thinly slice the cucumber.

Put the stock into a saucepan and bring to the boil. Add the remaining soy sauce, vinegar and salt. Put in the cucumber and simmer for 1 minute. Add the pork and simmer for a further 10 minutes.

CRAB SOUP

225g/8 oz crab meat
15g/½ oz fresh ginger root
2 spring onions
4 tbsp oil
¼ tsp salt
2 tbsp rice wine or dry sherry
900ml/1½ pints chicken stock
2 tsp cornflour
2 egg whites
2 tbsp chopped fresh coriander or parsley

Peel and slice the ginger root. Finely chop the spring onions. Heat the oil in a saucepan on a moderate heat. Add the ginger and onions and stir-fry them for 1 minute. Remove the ginger.

Put in the crab meat, salt and wine or sherry and stir-fry for 1 minute. Pour in the stock and bring to the boil. Simmer for 2 minutes. Lightly beat the cornflour with the egg whites and stir the mixture into the soup. Stir on a low heat for 2–3 minutes or until the soup thickens.

Pour the soup either into a large tureen or into individual bowls and garnish with the coriander or parsley.

FISH AND TOMATO SOUP

450g/1 lb white fish fillets
350g/12 oz tomatoes, scalded, skinned
    and chopped
1 tsp salt
1 tbsp cornflour
2 tbsp rice wine or dry sherry
900ml/1½ pints chicken stock
4 spring onions, finely chopped
1 tsp grated fresh ginger root
2 tbsp soy sauce
3 tbsp chopped fresh coriander or parsley

Cut the fish into 2.5cm/1in squares. Mix with the salt, cornflour and wine or sherry. Put the stock into a saucepan and bring to the boil. Put in the fish, tomatoes, spring onions, ginger root and soy sauce. Simmer, uncovered, for 5 minutes.

Stir in the coriander or parsley just before serving.

LIVER PÂTÉ SOUP

225g/8 oz pig's liver
2 egg whites
2 spring onions, finely chopped
1 tsp grated fresh ginger root
freshly ground black pepper
750ml/1¼ pints chicken stock
2 tbsp chopped fresh coriander or parsley

Finely mince the liver or purée it in a blender or food processor. Mix the liver with the egg whites, spring onions and ginger and season well with the pepper. Put the mixture into a serving bowl. Set the bowl on a rack over boiling water, cover and steam for 30 minutes or until the liver is firm. Cut the liver pâté into diamond shapes, leaving the pieces in the bowl.

Bring the stock to the boil and pour over the pâté. Garnish with coriander or parsley.

FISH AND SHELLFISH

With 2 main rivers and a long sea coast, China has a wealth of both freshwater and sea fish and of prawns, crabs and other shellfish.

A popular method of cooking fish to preserve all the natural flavour is to steam it, either whole or in fillets or steaks. Fish and soy sauce, both specialities of the coastal region, are combined to make the soy-flavoured dishes of red-cooked fish and smoked fish. The sugar smoking method from Szechuan usually applies to river fish but white sea fish works just as well. Sweet and sour fish is prepared in Hunan in the northern region.

Fish and shellfish are served around Canton and Phoenix tailed and barbequed prawns are served around the Yangtze Delta.

BARBEQUED PRAWNS

450g/1 lb prawns in shells
25g/1 oz fresh ginger root
4 tbsp rice wine or dry sherry
4 tbsp soy sauce
3 tbsp sesame oil
2 tsp Barbados sugar
1 garlic clove, crushed with a pinch of salt

Wash the prawns. Remove the legs but keep the heads and shells on. Peel and grate the ginger root and mix with the remaining ingredients. Turn the prawns in the mixture and leave for 30 minutes at room temperature.

Heat the oven to 200°C/400°F/Gas 6. Lay the prawns on a rack in a roasting tin and cook in the oven for 10 minutes. Cool completely before serving.

PHOENIX TAILED PRAWNS

450g/1 lb prawns in shells
2 tbsp rice wine or dry sherry
pinch of salt
1 egg
4 tbsp cornflour
4 tbsp water
oil for deep frying

ACCOMPANIMENTS
roasted salt and pepper
sweet soy bean sauce

Remove the heads from the prawns. Peel away the shells down to the last section and leave the tails on. Cut the prawns three-quarters of the way through, lengthways along the underside, and beat flat. Sprinkle with the wine or sherry and the salt and leave for 15 minutes.

Make a batter by beating together the egg, cornflour and water. Heat a pan of deep oil to 190°C/375°F. Holding the prawns by their tails, dip each one in the batter. Deep-fry for about 2 minutes, 6 at a time, until crisp. Drain on kitchen paper, keeping each batch warm in a low oven until they are all cooked. Serve the roasted salt and pepper and the sauce separately.

ROASTED SALT AND PEPPER
4 tbsp coarse salt
1 tbsp Szechuan peppercorns or black
** peppercorns**

Heat a heavy frying pan on a high heat. Put in the salt and pepper and turn the heat to moderate. Cook, stirring constantly, for 5 minutes or until the salt browns lightly.

Crush the mixture using a pestle and mortar or put between 2 sheets of greaseproof paper and crush with a rolling pin. Rub the mixture through a sieve. Use as a dip for the prawns.

STIR-FRIED PRAWNS WITH PEAS AND MUSHROOMS

450g/1 lb prawns in shells
2 tsp cornflour
1 egg white
1 tbsp rice wine or dry sherry
225g/8 oz button mushrooms
2 spring onions
4 tbsp oil
15g/½ oz fresh ginger root, sliced
225g/8 oz cooked peas

Shell the prawns and coat in the cornflour. Put the prawns into a bowl and mix in the egg white and wine or sherry. Leave to marinate for 30 minutes. Thinly slice the mushrooms. Cut the spring onions into 2.5cm/1in lengths.

Heat the oil and ginger root in a wok or large frying pan on a high heat. Stir-fry the ginger root for 30 seconds and remove it. Put in the mushrooms and spring onions and stir-fry for 1 minute. Put in the prawns and stir-fry for 2 minutes or until they turn pink. Mix in the peas and stir-fry for 1 minute to heat through.

★ *The ginger root may be omitted if it is not available.*

STIR-FRIED PRAWNS WITH TOMATOES IN RED HOT SAUCE

225g/8 oz shelled prawns
350g/12 oz tomatoes
15g/½ oz fresh ginger root
2 tbsp tomato purée
1 tbsp cornflour
4 tbsp cold water
4 tbsp oil
1 garlic clove, finely chopped
4 spring onions, finely chopped
1 tbsp rice wine or dry sherry
1 tbsp chilli sauce

Cut the tomatoes into wedges. Peel and grate the ginger root. Mix together the tomato purée, cornflour and water.

Heat the oil in a wok or large frying pan on a high heat. Put in the ginger, garlic and spring onions and stir-fry for about 15 seconds. Add the prawns and stir-fry for 1½ minutes or until they turn pink and firm. Mix in the tomatoes and cook for 30 seconds. Add the wine or sherry, chilli sauce and cornflour mixture. Cook, stirring, until the liquid thickens to a glaze.

CRAB WITH EGGS

225g/8 oz crab meat
100g/4 oz mushrooms
50g/2 oz tinned water chestnuts
50g/2 oz bamboo shoots
4 spring onions
4 eggs
2 tbsp soy sauce
40g/1½ oz lard
2 tbsp chopped fresh coriander

Shred the crab meat. Thinly slice the mushrooms. Cut the water chestnuts and bamboo shoots into matchstick pieces. Cut the spring onions into 2.5cm/1in lengths. Beat the eggs with the soy sauce. Mix in the crab, mushrooms, water chestnuts, bamboo shoots and onions.

Heat the lard in a wok or large frying pan on a moderate heat. Stir in the egg mixture and keep stirring until it scrambles. Pile the scramble into a warmed serving dish and scatter the coriander over the top.

★ Parsley may be used if coriander is not available.

STEAMED FISH FILLETS WITH BLACK BEAN SAUCE

675g/1½ lb white fish fillets
15g/½ oz fresh ginger root
1 garlic clove, crushed with a pinch of salt
4 spring onions, finely chopped
2 tbsp black bean paste
2 tbsp sesame oil

Cut the fish into even-sized pieces. Peel and grate the ginger root and mix with the remaining ingredients. Put the fish fillets onto a dish and spoon over the ginger mixture.

Steam the fish, covered, over simmering water for 10 minutes or until cooked through.

STEAMED FISH IN HOT SAUCE

one 675-g/1½-lb trout or other freshwater
   fish
salt and freshly ground black pepper
25g/1 oz fresh ginger root
4 spring onions
1 tbsp oil
1 garlic clove, finely chopped
1 tbsp chilli sauce
1 tbsp tomato purée
2 tbsp soy sauce
150ml/¼ pint chicken stock
1 tbsp cornflour mixed with 4 tbsp water

Clean the trout and cut off the fins. Leave the head
and tail on. Make 2 diagonal slashes on each side of
the fish, running downwards and backwards from
head to tail. Season the trout well, inside and out,
and place on a flat dish. Put one half of the ginger
and spring onions inside the fish and one half on
top. Mix together the oil, garlic, chilli sauce,
tomato purée, soy sauce and stock. Pour the
mixture over the trout.

Bring some water to the boil in a large wok. Put a
stand in the wok. Place the trout dish on the stand.
Cover and steam for 30 minutes or until the fish is
cooked through.

Lift the trout onto a serving plate. Pour the liquid
from the dish into a saucepan. Bring to the boil and
stir in the cornflour mixture. Simmer, stirring,
until you have a thick sauce. Pour the sauce over the
fish.

SWEET AND SOUR FISH

450g/1 lb whiting fillets
oil for deep frying

SAUCE
1 medium carrot
1 green pepper
15g/½ oz fresh ginger root
1 tbsp cornflour
200ml/7 fl oz chicken stock
1 tbsp Barbados sugar
1 tbsp white wine vinegar
2 tbsp oil

COATING
25g/1 oz cornflour
2 egg whites
1 tbsp rice wine or dry sherry

Cut each whiting fillet in half crossways. To make
the sauce, first cut the carrot and the pepper into
matchstick pieces. Peel and grate the ginger root.
Put the cornflour into a bowl and gradually stir in
the chicken stock. Add the sugar and vinegar.

Heat the oil in a wok or frying pan on a high heat.
Put in the carrot, pepper and ginger root and stir-
fry for 1½ minutes. Add the cornflour and stock
mixture. Bring to the boil, stirring, and stir until
you have a thick sauce. Keep the sauce warm.

For the coating, put the cornflour into a bowl and
gradually mix in the egg whites and wine or sherry.
Heat a pan of deep oil to 160°C/325°F. Dip the fish
pieces into the coating and deep-fry about 4 at a
time until they are golden brown. Drain on kitchen
paper.

Put the fish onto a warmed serving dish and pour
the sweet and sour sauce over the top.

RED-COOKED FISH STEAKS

4 cod or halibut steaks
1 tsp salt
2 tbsp cornflour
25g/1 oz fresh ginger root
4 spring onions
4 tbsp oil
3 tbsp soy sauce
3 tbsp rice wine or dry sherry
100ml/3 fl oz chicken stock

Skin the fish steaks and rub with the salt and corn-flour. Peel and finely chop the ginger root. Cut the spring onions into 2.5cm/1 in lengths.

Heat the oil in a wok or frying pan on a high heat. Put in the ginger and spring onions and stir-fry for 30 seconds. Add the fish steaks and brown on each side. Pour in the soy sauce, wine or sherry and chicken stock.

Bring the stock to the boil. Cover and simmer gently for 10 minutes.

SPICED CRISP FISH

4 small trout
15g/½ oz fresh ginger root
6 tbsp soy sauce
2 tbsp rice wine or sherry
¼ tsp aniseeds
25g/1 oz flour
oil for deep frying

Clean the trout and cut off the fins. Keep the heads and tails on. Peel and grate the ginger root and mix with the soy sauce, wine or sherry and aniseeds. Brush the trout with the mixture and leave for 2 hours at room temperature. Brush the trout dry and rub with the flour. Leave for a further 30 minutes.

Heat a pan of deep oil to 180°C/350°F. Deep-fry the fish, one at a time, until the skins are brown and crisp. Drain the trout on kitchen paper and serve hot.

SMOKED FISH

675g/1½ lb firm white fish fillets
15g/½ oz fresh ginger root, peeled and finely
** chopped**
4 tbsp rice wine or dry sherry
2 tbsp soy sauce
2 spring onions, finely chopped
1 garlic clove, finely chopped
½ tsp five-spice powder
2 tbsp brown sugar
oil for deep frying
150ml/¼ pint stock or water
1 tbsp cornflour

Cut the fish into 2.5cm/1in cubes. Mix the ginger root with the wine or sherry, soy sauce, spring onions, garlic, five-spice powder and sugar. Mix the fish into the marinade and leave for 1 hour at room temperature. Lift out the fish and reserve the marinade.

Heat a pan of deep oil to 180°C/350°F. Add the pieces of fish and fry until they are golden brown. Lift out the fish and drain on kitchen paper.

Mix the marinade with the stock or water and cornflour. Put the mixture into a saucepan and bring to the boil, stirring. Stir until you have a thick sauce. Put the pieces of fried fish into the sauce and leave until they are completely cool. The fish can then be served cold or reheated in a warm oven.

SUGAR-SMOKED FISH

675g/1½ lb firm white fish fillets
3 tbsp soy sauce
½ tsp salt
4 tbsp oil
3 tbsp Barbados sugar

Cut the fish into 5cm/2in square pieces. Sprinkle with the soy sauce, salt and oil and leave for 1 hour at room temperature.

Heat the oven to 220°C/425°F/Gas 7. Line a baking tin with foil and sprinkle in the brown sugar. Put a rack into the tin and put the fish on the rack. Cover the tin completely with foil and cook in the oven for 10 minutes. Serve immediately.

PORK

Pork is the most commonly used meat in Chinese cooking and it is a great favourite in the coastal region. From here comes the simple white-cooked pork, rich, steamed pork with ground rice, red-cooked pork and the delicious Lions' Heads, a casserole of savoury meat balls made from pork and shrimps or prawns simmered on top of Chinese cabbage. The name comes from the appearance of the dish, the meat balls being the heads and the cabbage the mane.

Sweet and sour pork from Canton and spiced spare ribs from Szechuan are both dishes that are popular in the West. Ham is also a Szechuan speciality. Pork kidneys are often served cold with a spiced sauce.

SWEET AND SOUR PORK WITH PINEAPPLE

675g/1½ lb pork belly
1 tsp salt
1 tbsp dry sherry
1 tbsp cornflour
1 egg, beaten
oil for deep frying

SAUCE
3 slices fresh pineapple
2 medium carrots
1 green pepper
1 medium onion
3 tbsp oil
1 garlic clove, finely chopped
100ml/3½ fl oz chicken stock
100ml/3½ fl oz pineapple juice
2 tbsp white wine vinegar
1 tbsp cornflour mixed with 4 tbsp cold water

Cut the rind and bones from the pork. Cut the meat into 2cm/¾in pieces. Put the pork pieces into a bowl, sprinkle in the salt and sherry and leave for 30 minutes. Put the cornflour into a bowl and beat in the egg to make a batter. Stir the batter into the pork.

To make the sauce, first core and dice the slices of pineapple. Cut the carrots into matchstick pieces. Core and seed the pepper and cut into 2cm/¾in squares. Finely chop the onion.

Heat the oil in a wok or frying pan on a high heat. Add the garlic and vegetables and stir-fry for 2 minutes. Add the pineapple pieces and stir-fry for 1 minute. Pour in the stock, pineapple juice and vinegar. Stir in the cornflour mixture and bring the sauce to the boil, stirring. Stir until the sauce thickens and becomes clear. Keep the sauce warm.

Heat a pan of deep oil to 180°C/350°F. Put in the pork pieces and fry until they are golden brown. Remove and drain on kitchen paper. Add the pork pieces to the sauce and simmer for 1 minute.

STIR-FRIED PORK WITH GINGER

900g/2 lb belly pork
2 tbsp cornflour
2 tbsp oil
100ml/3½ fl oz dry sherry
50ml/1½ fl oz soy sauce
25g/1 oz fresh ginger root, peeled and grated
2 medium onions, finely chopped
1 garlic clove, finely chopped

Cut the pork into small dice-sized pieces and coat in the cornflour. Heat the oil in a wok or large frying pan on a high heat. Put in the pork and stir-fry for about 4 minutes until brown and crisp. Pour off any excess fat.

Put the wok or pan back onto a medium heat and pour in the sherry and soy sauce. Bring to the boil. Add the ginger root, onions and garlic and stir-fry for 2 minutes more.

PORK WITH ASPARAGUS

450g/1 lb lean, boneless pork
350g/12 oz asparagus
1 tbsp cornflour
1 tbsp soy sauce
1 tbsp rice wine or dry sherry
200ml/7 fl oz chicken stock
4 tbsp oil
1 garlic clove, finely chopped
1 small onion, finely chopped

Cut the pork into small thin slivers. Cut the asparagus into 2.5cm/1in slices, put into boiling water and cook for 4 minutes. Drain. Put the cornflour into a bowl and mix in the soy sauce, wine or sherry and stock.

Heat the oil in a wok or large frying pan on a high heat. Put in the pork and garlic. Stir-fry for 4–5 minutes until the pork browns and all the moisture in the pan has been driven away.

Add the onion, lower the heat and stir-fry for 1 minute. Put in the asparagus and stir-fry for 1 minute more. Stir the cornflour mixture and pour into the pan. Cook, stirring, until it thickens to a glossy sauce.

★ Instead of asparagus, blanched cauliflower florets may be used, or 2.5cm/1in lengths of peeled, seeded but uncooked cucumber.

CHA SHAO (ROAST PORK STRIPS)

900g/2 lb lean, boneless pork (fillet or shoulder)
4 tbsp chicken stock
1 tbsp yellow bean sauce
3 tbsp soy sauce
3 tbsp Kao Liang spirit or brandy
2 tbsp Barbados sugar
2 tbsp honey, melted

Cut the pork into long strips about 4cm/1½in wide. Lay the strips in a shallow dish. Mix together the stock, yellow bean and soy sauces, the spirit or brandy and the sugar. Pour the mixture over the pork. Marinate for 3 hours at room temperature, turning the pork from time to time.

Heat the oven to 200°C/400°F/Gas 6. Lay the strips of pork on a rack in a roasting tin. Pour about 2.5cm/1in of water into the base of the tin, not touching the pork. Roast the pork for 30 minutes. Baste with the honey and return to the oven for 10 minutes.

Cool the pork completely and serve cut into very thin slices. Any left over can be used as part of the filling for steamed buns or spring rolls or used for an omelette.

RED-COOKED PORK

one 1.8-kg/4-lb joint hand of pork or
    knuckle end leg of pork
175g/6 oz dried chestnuts
8 dried Chinese mushrooms
300ml/½ pint water
6 tbsp soy sauce
4 tbsp rice wine or dry sherry
2 tsp Barbados sugar
1 piece star anise
4 spring onions, cut into 7.5cm/3in lengths
1 garlic clove, finely chopped

Keep the rind on the pork. Soak the chestnuts and
the mushrooms in warm water for 1 hour. Put the
pork into a large casserole and cover with cold
water. Bring to the boil, boil for 5 minutes and
drain. Run cold water over the pork, drain again
and return to the casserole.

Mix together the 300ml/½ pint of water, soy
sauce, wine or sherry and sugar. Pour the mixture
over the pork. Add the star anise, spring onions and
garlic. Bring to the boil, cover and simmer on the
lowest heat possible for 2 hours, turning the meat
several times. Add the mushrooms and chestnuts
and simmer for a further 30 minutes.

Put the pork into a warmed, deep dish and pour
any remaining sauce over it. Surround with the
chestnuts and mushrooms.

As one meal this will serve 6–8 people. Any left
over can be put into dumplings or spring or egg
rolls, or used for an omelette.

SIMMERED PORK WITH EGGS

450g/1 lb lean, boneless pork
2 spring onions
2 tbsp oil
6 tbsp soy sauce
4 tbsp rice wine or dry sherry
1 tsp Barbados sugar
½ tsp ground ginger
350ml/12 fl oz water
4 hard-boiled eggs, shelled
2 tbsp chopped fresh coriander or parsley

Cut the pork into 2.5cm/1in cubes. Cut the spring
onions into 2.5cm/1in lengths. Heat the oil in a
wok or casserole on a high heat. Put in the pork and
brown it. Add the spring onions, soy sauce, wine
or sherry, sugar and ginger. Pour in the water and
stir. Cover and simmer on a very low heat for
45 minutes. Put in the whole eggs, cover again and
simmer for a further 20 minutes.

To serve, take out the eggs. Lift the pork into a
warmed serving dish. Cut the eggs in half lengthways and arrange around and on top of the pork.
Scatter over the coriander or parsley before
serving.

WHITE-COOKED PORK

900-g/2-lb piece leg of pork
15g/½ oz fresh ginger root
4 spring onions

SAUCE
15g/½ oz fresh ginger root
3 spring onions
4 tbsp soy sauce
1 tbsp Kao Liang spirit or brandy
1 tbsp sesame oil
1 tbsp black bean sauce

Bone the pork and cut off the rind. Roll and tie the meat, put into a large saucepan or casserole and cover with cold water. Add the ginger and the spring onions. Set on a moderate heat and bring to the boil. Skim, cover and simmer for 1 hour 30 minutes or until the pork is completely tender. Take out the pork and leave, covered, for 8 hours to cool.

To serve, cut off all but 2mm/¹⁄₁₀in of fat from the pork and cut the meat, across the grain, into very thin slices. Arrange the slices on a serving plate.

To make the sauce, peel and grate the ginger root and finely chop the spring onions. Mix them with the remaining ingredients. The sauce may be poured over the pork or served separately as a dip.

SZECHUAN TWICE-COOKED PORK

1.125kg/2½ lb loin of pork, in one piece
15g/½ oz fresh ginger root
2 tbsp oil
1 garlic clove, peeled and bruised
1 spring onion, finely chopped
2 tbsp soy sauce
1 tbsp chilli sauce

Put the pork into a saucepan and cover with water. Bring to the boil, skim and simmer for 1 hour. Take out the meat and cool completely. Remove the bones and cut the meat into 6-mm/¼-in thick slices.

Peel and finely chop the ginger root. Heat the oil and garlic in a wok or frying pan on a high heat. Remove the garlic as soon as it begins to brown. Add the pork, spring onion, soy sauce and chilli sauce and cook, stirring for 5 minutes, lowering the heat if necessary so the pork is heated through.

LIONS' HEADS

450g/1 lb pork, about one-quarter fat
50g/2 oz shelled prawns
4 tinned water chestnuts
2 spring onions
1 tsp grated fresh ginger root
3 tbsp soy sauce
2 tbsp rice wine or dry sherry
2 tbsp cornflour
125ml/4 fl oz chicken stock
450g/1 lb Chinese cabbage
3 tbsp oil

Mince the pork. Finely chop the prawns, water chestnuts and spring onions and mix into the pork. Beat in the ginger root, 2 tbsp soy sauce and the wine or sherry. Form the mixture into 4 round balls. Mix together the cornflour and 3 tbsp of the chicken stock. Roll the pork balls in the mixture.

Cut the Chinese cabbage into lengthways quarters. Cut each quarter in half crossways and then separate the leaves. Put half the cabbage into the bottom of a flameproof casserole.

Heat the oil in a frying pan or wok on a medium heat. Put in the pork balls and brown them all over. Add the pork balls to the casserole and put the remaining Chinese cabbage on top. Mix together the remaining soy sauce and stock and pour over the cabbage.

Set the casserole on a high heat and bring the stock to the boil. Cover and cook on a very low heat for 30 minutes.

Serve the Lions' heads on a bed of cabbage.

STEAMED PORK WITH GROUND RICE

450g/1 lb pork belly, in one piece
3 tbsp soy sauce
2 tbsp rice wine or dry sherry
2 tbsp chicken stock
100g/4 oz ground rice
1 piece star anise
4 sprigs fresh coriander or parsley

Bone the pork but leave the rind on. Cut the meat into small, oblong pieces about 10cm/4in long. Mix together the soy sauce, wine or sherry and stock. Marinate the pork in the mixture for 30 minutes.

Put the ground rice into a large, heavy frying pan with the star anise. Set the pan on a moderate heat, stirring for about 5 minutes until the rice begins to brown. Remove the star anise and tip the rice onto a plate to cool.

Coat the pieces of pork in the rice. Put the pieces into a basin, skin-side down and pour in any remaining marinade. Cover the basin with grease-proof paper and foil, tying them securely. Bring a large pan of water to the boil. Lower in the basin, cover the pan and steam the pork for 2 hours or until it is very tender.

To serve, turn the pork onto a warmed serving dish and garnish with the sprigs of coriander or parsley.

DEEP-FRIED SPICED SPARE RIBS

900g/2 lb pork spare ribs
3 tbsp soy sauce
3 tbsp rice wine or dry sherry
½ tsp five-spice powder
15g/½ oz fresh ginger root, peeled and
   chopped
½ tsp freshly ground Szechuan pepper or
   black pepper
pinch of salt
1 egg, beaten
2 tsp cornflour
oil for deep frying
1 tbsp chilli sauce

Put the spare ribs into a dish and sprinkle with 1 tbsp each of the soy sauce and wine or sherry, the five-spice powder, ginger, pepper and salt. Turn the spare ribs and leave for 1 hour at room temperature. Beat the egg with the cornflour and pour the resulting batter over the spare ribs. Turn the spare ribs to coat them.

Heat a pan of deep oil to 180°C/350°F. Add the spare ribs and fry until they are crisp and golden. Remove and drain on kitchen paper.

Mix together the remaining sauce and sherry and the chilli sauce. Heat a frying pan or wok on a moderate heat. Put in the cooked spare ribs and stir in the sauce mixture.

Stir-fry for 15 seconds and then lift the spare ribs into a serving dish.

HAM WITH PEPPERS

450g/1 lb lean cooked ham, in one piece
1 tbsp cornflour
2 tbsp soy sauce
2 tbsp dry sherry
2 tbsp chicken stock
2 red peppers
2 green peppers
3 tbsp oil

Cut the ham into pieces about 6mm/¼ in thick and 2.5cm/1 in square. Mix together the cornflour, soy sauce, sherry and stock. Stir in the ham strips to coat them with the mixture. Core and seed the peppers and cut into 2.5cm/1 in strips.

Heat the oil in a wok or large frying pan on a high heat. Put in the peppers and stir-fry for 1 minute. Add the ham and stir-fry for 3 minutes so both ham and peppers become coated in a thick glaze.

STEAMED HAM WITH PINEAPPLE

450g/1 lb pressed ham, thinly sliced
1 small pineapple
3 tbsp honey

Cut the slices of ham into small pieces about 2.5 × 4cm/1 × 1½ in. Cut the husk from the pineapple. Cut the flesh into rings. Core and chop the rings and cut into 1cm/½ in pieces.

Line 2 small basins with about two-thirds of the ham and fill with the pineapple. Spoon ½ tbsp honey into each one. Cover the pineapple with the remaining ham. Cover each basin with greaseproof paper and foil. Stand the basins on a rack over boiling water and steam the ham for 30 minutes.

Lift out the basins and remove the greaseproof and foil. Invert a plate over each one. Hold each basin and plate close together and pour off as much liquid as possible. Clean the plates, invert them over the bowls again and turn out the ham.

Melt the remaining honey and spoon over the top.

PORK KIDNEY SALAD

4 pork kidneys
300ml/½ pint water
2 tbsp rice wine or dry sherry
3 tbsp oil
15g/½ oz fresh ginger root, peeled and grated
4 spring onions, finely chopped
1 garlic clove, finely chopped
2 tbsp soy sauce
2 tsp white wine vinegar
1 tsp sugar
½ tsp chilli sauce
1 tbsp sesame oil

Cut the kidneys in half lengthways. Cut out the centre cores. With a sharp knife, make a diamond patterned scoring on the outside of the kidney halves. Then cut each half into paper-thin slices. Soak the kidneys in cold water for 1 hour, changing the water twice. Drain well.

Put the water and wine or sherry into a saucepan and bring to the boil. Add the kidneys and cook for about 2 minutes or until they change colour. Using a perforated spoon, lift them out of the pan immediately.

Heat the oil in a wok or large frying pan on a high heat. Put in the ginger, spring onions and garlic and stir-fry for 1 minute. Add the kidneys, soy sauce, vinegar, sugar and chilli sauce.

Stir-fry for 30 seconds so the kidneys heat through. Take the pan from the heat and stir in the sesame oil.

Transfer the kidneys and sauce to a serving dish. Cool to room temperature before serving.

BEEF

Beef is a speciality in the western regions of Szechuan and Yunnan and from here come the lightly flavoured stewed beef which can be served hot or cold and spiced fried beef. Deep-fried beef is a speciality of the northern region and beef in oyster sauce and pepper steak comes from Canton.

STIR-FRIED BEEF WITH MIXED VEGETABLES

450g/1 lb rump steak
2 tsp cornflour
2 tbsp soy sauce
1 tbsp rice wine or dry sherry
100g/4 oz mange tout peas
half 225-g/8-oz tin bamboo shoots
100g/4 oz mushrooms
1 small onion
15g/½ oz fresh ginger root
3 tbsp oil
100g/4 oz bean sprouts

Cut the beef into small, thin slivers. Mix together the cornflour, soy sauce and dry sherry. Stir in the beef and leave to marinate for 30 minutes.

Top and tail the mange tout peas. Put the peas into boiling water, cook for 4 minutes and drain. Rinse through with cold water and drain again. Thinly slice the bamboo shoots and the mush-rooms. Thinly slice the onion. Peel and thinly slice the ginger root.

Heat 2 tbsp of the oil in a wok or frying pan on a high heat. Put in the mange tout peas, bamboo shoots, mushrooms, onion and bean sprouts. Stir-fry for 2 minutes and remove from the heat. Add the remaining oil and put in the ginger. Stir-fry for 15 seconds and add the beef slivers. Stir-fry for 2–3 minutes or until the beef is browned. Remove the ginger. Return the vegetables to the pan and stir-fry for 30 seconds to heat through.

★ *Broccoli may be used instead of mange tout peas.*

PEPPER STEAK

450g/1 lb rump or sirloin steak
2 green peppers
1 large onion
1 tbsp cornflour
2 tbsp soy sauce
150ml/¼ pint chicken stock
4 tbsp oil
1 tsp ground ginger

Cut the steak into small, thin slivers. Core and seed the peppers and cut into 1cm/½ in dice. Finely chop the onion. Mix together the cornflour, soy sauce and stock.

Heat the oil in a wok or large frying pan on a high heat. Add the beef and stir-fry until it browns and all the moisture in the pan has been driven away. Put in the peppers and onion and sprinkle in the ginger. Lower the heat and stir-fry for 2 minutes. Stir the cornflour mixture and pour into the wok or pan. Stir until it thickens to a translucent sauce and remove the pan from the heat.

STIR-FRIED BEEF IN OYSTER SAUCE

450g/1 lb fillet steak
1 tsp cornflour
½ tsp ground ginger
2 tbsp soy sauce
2 tbsp rice wine or dry sherry
4 spring onions
3 tbsp oil
125ml/4 fl oz stock
2 tbsp oyster sauce

Cut the fillet across the grain into very thin slices. Mix together the cornflour, ginger, soy sauce and wine or sherry. Mix in the beef and leave to marinate for 1 hour at room temperature. Finely chop the spring onions.

Heat the oil in a wok or large frying pan on a high heat. Add the beef, stir-fry for 1 minute and remove from the wok or pan. Put the onions into the pan and stir-fry for 30 seconds. Return the beef to the pan and pour in the stock and oyster sauce. Stir until it thickens to a glaze and remove the pan from the heat.

SPICED FRIED BEEF WITH LEEKS AND CELERY

450g/1 lb rump or sirloin steak
2 medium leeks
3 celery sticks
6 tbsp oil
1 garlic clove, crushed with a pinch of salt
1 tsp red wine vinegar
1 tsp soy sauce
1 tbsp sesame oil
1 tbsp hot soy bean paste

Cut the beef into small, thin slivers. Cut the leeks and celery into matchstick pieces.

Heat 3 tbsp oil in a wok or large frying pan on a high heat. Put in the leeks and celery. Stir-fry for 1 minute and remove. Add the remaining oil to the pan. Put in the steak and stir-fry until it has browned and all the moisture in the pan has evaporated. Stir in the garlic, vinegar, soy sauce, sesame oil and soy bean paste. Add the vegetables and stir-fry for 1 minute.

CHINESE STEWED BEEF

900g/2 lb stewing beef, in one piece
2 tbsp oil
4 spring onions
15g/½ oz fresh ginger root
6 tbsp soy sauce
2 tbsp rice wine or dry sherry
1 tbsp whole black peppercorns
1 tsp five-spice powder
water to cover
2 tsp cornflour mixed with 2 tbsp water

Heat the oil in a wok or large frying pan. Add the beef and brown all over. Remove the beef. Cut the spring onions into 2.5cm/1in lengths. Peel and thinly slice the ginger root.

Put the beef into a saucepan with the spring onions, ginger, soy sauce, wine or sherry, peppercorns and five-spice powder. Pour in water to just cover the meat. Bring the meat to the boil on a high heat. Cover and simmer very gently for 2 hours 30 minutes or until the beef is very tender.

Take out the beef. Cut into thick slices, put onto a serving dish and keep warm in the oven. Stir the cornflour mixture into the liquid remaining in the saucepan. Bring the liquid to the boil again, stirring until it becomes a thick, translucent sauce. Pour the sauce over the beef to serve.

★ *The beef can also be cooled completely, cut into small, thin slices and served cold with the same sauce as for white-cooked pork (p. 28).*

STEAMED BEEF AND PEPPERS

450g/1 lb lean braising steak
25g/1 oz dried Chinese mushrooms
150ml/¼ pint stock, boiling
1 red pepper
1 green pepper
1 medium onion, thinly sliced
1 garlic clove, finely chopped
1 tsp cornflour
3 tbsp soy sauce
2 tbsp sesame oil
1 tsp ground ginger
4–6 Chinese cabbage leaves

Cut the beef into small, thin slices. Put the mushrooms into a bowl, pour on the stock and leave for 20 minutes. Drain the mushrooms and reserve the stock.

Core and seed the peppers and cut into 2.5cm/1in strips. In a bowl, combine the beef, peppers, mushrooms, onion and garlic. Mix together the mushroom stock, cornflour, soy sauce, oil and ground ginger and add to the beef.

Line the top of a bamboo steamer with the cabbage leaves. Put in the beef mixture. Cover.

Bring a small amount of water to the boil in a wok or saucepan. Put in a trivet or stand and set the steamer on top. Cover and steam for 1 hour 15 minutes or until the beef is quite tender. Serve straight from the steamer.

MINCED BEEF PEARL BALLS

225g/8 oz short grain rice
575g/1¼ lb minced beef
½ tsp salt
¼ tsp freshly ground black pepper
6 tinned water chestnuts
6 spring onions
15g/½ oz fresh ginger root
2 tbsp black bean sauce
1½ tbsp cornflour
2 tbsp rice wine or dry sherry
2 tbsp water or stock
soy sauce for serving

Soak the rice in cold water for 2 hours. Drain the rice and spread on a flat tray or on greaseproof paper. Put the beef into a large mixing bowl and add the salt and pepper. Finely chop the water chestnuts and spring onions. Peel and finely chop the ginger root. Add them to the beef, together with the black bean sauce. Mix the cornflour with the wine or sherry and stock or water. Add the liquid to the beef and mix well.

Form the mixture into small balls about 2cm/¾ in in diameter. Roll the balls in the rice, making sure that they are well covered. Press extra rice round them using your fingers.

Put the meat balls into a steamer in not more than 2 layers. Set over boiling water, cover and steam for 30 minutes.

Remove the meat balls to a serving dish and serve the soy sauce separately as a dip.

STEAMED BEEF AND CHINESE VEGETABLES

25g/1 oz dried Chinese mushrooms
150ml/¼ pint stock, boiling
450g/1 lb lean topside of beef
one 225-g/8-oz tin water chestnuts
one 225-g/8-oz tin bamboo shoots
1 tsp cornflour
2 tsp soy sauce
2 tbsp dry sherry
1 tbsp oil
1 tbsp white wine vinegar
4–6 Chinese cabbage leaves
1 medium onion, finely chopped
15g/½ oz fresh ginger root, peeled and grated

Pour the stock over the mushrooms and leave for 20 minutes. Drain the mushrooms and reserve the stock. Cut the beef into small, thin slices. Drain and thinly slice the water chestnuts and bamboo shoots. Mix the reserved stock with the cornflour, soy sauce, sherry, oil and vinegar.

Line a bamboo steamer with the Chinese cabbage leaves. Mix together the mushrooms, beef, water chestnuts, bamboo shoots, onion and ginger root and put the mixture into the steamer. Cover.

Bring a small amount of water to the boil in a wok or a large saucepan. Put in a trivet or stand and set the steamer on top. Cover and steam the beef mixture for 1 hour 15 minutes or until the beef is quite tender. Serve straight from the steamer.

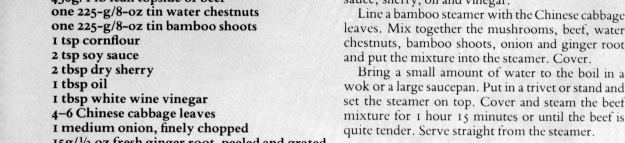

DEEP-FRIED BEEF WITH DIPS

450g/1 lb rump or sirloin steak
4 tbsp soy sauce
1 tbsp hoisin sauce
15g/½ oz fresh ginger root, peeled and grated
6 spring onions
2 tbsp cornflour
2 egg whites
oil for deep frying

YELLOW BEAN DIP
3 tbsp yellow bean paste
1 tsp chilli sauce
2 tbsp soy sauce

BLACK BEAN DIP
4 tbsp hot black bean paste
4 tbsp soy sauce

TOMATO AND CHILLI DIP
1 tbsp tomato purée
1 tsp chilli sauce
4 tbsp soy sauce

SOY AND SESAME DIP
1 tbsp sesame paste
2 tbsp soy sauce
2 tbsp sesame oil
1 tbsp white wine vinegar

Ask your butcher to slice the steak very thinly. Cut each slice into pieces about 5 × 2.5cm/2 × 1in. Mix together the soy sauce, hoisin sauce and ginger root. Put in the beef and stir to coat all over with the sauce. Leave for 1 hour at room temperature. Mix the ingredients for each dip separately and put into small bowls for serving. Cut the spring onions into matchstick pieces.

Beat together the cornflour and egg whites. Heat a pan of deep oil to 180°C/350°F. Dip the pieces of beef in the batter and fry, about 4 at a time, until they are golden brown. Drain on kitchen paper and keep hot while you cook the rest. Lay the beef on a warmed dish and surround with the spring onions.

LAMB

Most of the Chinese lamb dishes come from the northern area around the city of Peking. The twice-cooked lamb and barbequed lamb are variations of recipes that came originally from the Mongols. The barbequed lamb is often cooked in the winter over large braziers round which the diners can warm themselves.

Jellied lamb can be served with a selection of other cold meats either as the main part of the meal or as an appetizer.

The steamed and then deep-fried breast of lamb makes a tasty and economical family meal and the lamb in yellow bean sauce is warming and spicy.

CLEAR SIMMERED LAMB

900g/2 lb lean, boneless lamb, leg or shoulder
4 spring onions
25g/1 oz fresh ginger root
6 tbsp soy sauce
300ml/½ pint chicken stock
6 tbsp rice wine or dry sherry

Cut the lamb into 2.5cm/1 in cubes. Cut the spring onions into 2.5cm/1 in lengths. Peel and grate the ginger root. Put the lamb, spring onions and ginger root into a casserole and add the soy sauce, chicken stock and wine or sherry. Bring to the boil. Cover and simmer gently for 1 hour 30 minutes.

Serve with plain boiled or steamed rice and a vegetable dish.

TWICE-COOKED LEG OF LAMB

1 small leg of lamb
4 tbsp soy sauce
2 tbsp black bean paste
2 tbsp hoisin sauce
1 tbsp chilli sauce
1 tsp five-spice powder
4 garlic cloves, crushed
25g/1 oz fresh ginger root, peeled and grated
300ml/½ pint dry red wine
1.2 litres/2 pints chicken stock
3 tbsp sesame oil
6 spring onions, shredded

HOISIN DIP
4 tbsp hoisin sauce
4 tbsp soy sauce
4 tbsp rice wine or dry sherry

CHILLI DIP
2 tsp chilli sauce
6 tbsp soy sauce
2 tbsp red wine vinegar

In a saucepan, mix together the soy sauce, black bean paste, hoisin and chilli sauces, five-spice powder, garlic cloves, ginger root, wine and stock. Bring to the boil, cover and simmer for 45 minutes. Put the lamb into a large casserole and pour the hot sauce over the top. Set the casserole on a low heat and simmer for 1 hour. Cool the lamb in the liquid for 8 hours.

Heat the oven to 180°C/350°F/Gas 4. Put the lamb on a rack in a roasting tin and brush with the sesame oil. Cook in the oven for 1 hour or until brown and tender. Cut the lamb into small, fairly thick slices and arrange on a serving plate. Garnish with the spring onions.

While the lamb is cooking mix together the ingredients for the separate dips and put each one into a small bowl. Serve the dips alongside the plate of lamb.

JELLIED LAMB

**675g/1½ lb lean, boneless lamb, leg or
shoulder, cut into 2.5cm/1 in cubes
4 garlic cloves, peeled and bruised
1 tsp salt
4 tbsp soy sauce
4 tbsp rice wine or dry sherry
1 whole star anise
25g/1 oz gelatine
6 tbsp cold water
2 spring onions
oil for greasing**

Put the lamb into a saucepan with the garlic, salt,
soy sauce, wine or sherry and star anise. Add
enough cold water to cover. Bring to the boil and
skim. Cover and cook on a low heat for 2 hours or
until the lamb is very tender. Drain. Discard the
garlic and star anise and reserve the cooking liquid.

Soak the gelatine in the cold water. Chop the
spring onions or cut into short lengths. Make a
pattern with them in the bottom of a greased
900g/2 lb loaf tin. Put the reserved cooking liquid
into a saucepan and reheat without boiling. Stir in
the soaked gelatine and go on stirring until it
dissolves. Cool the liquid, pour a little over the
spring onions and put the loaf tin into the refrigerator to set the spring onions in place.

Mix the lamb with the remaining liquid and pour
into the loaf tin. Leave the jelly in a cool place to set
completely. Turn out and serve.

LAMB IN YELLOW BEAN SAUCE

**575g/1¼ lb boned leg of lamb
1 tbsp cornflour
2 tbsp soy sauce
2 tbsp yellow bean sauce
1 tbsp hoisin sauce
1 tbsp white wine vinegar
1 tsp grated fresh ginger root
100ml/3½ fl oz chicken stock
3 tbsp oil**

Cut the lamb into small, thin slivers and lightly
coat with half the cornflour. Mix the remaining
cornflour with the sauces, vinegar, ginger root and
chicken stock.

Heat the oil in a wok or large frying pan on a high
heat. Add the lamb and stir-fry until browned and
any moisture in the pan has evaporated.

Stir the cornflour mixture and add to the pan.
Bring to the boil and stir until it thickens.

CRISPED BREAST OF LAMB

900-g/2-lb breast of lamb
1 tbsp Szechuan or black peppercorns
½ tbsp salt
15g/½ oz fresh ginger root
2 tbsp soy sauce
oil for deep frying
dips as for deep-fried beef (p. 39)

Chop the lamb into pieces about 7.5 × 2.5cm/ 3 × 1 in. Put the peppercorns and salt into a heavy saucepan and set on a moderate heat. Stir for 3 minutes and tip out to cool. Crush the peppercorns coarsely. Peel and grate the ginger root. Put the lamb into a bowl and add the salt and pepper mixture, the ginger and the soy sauce. Turn to coat.

Put the lamb into a steamer and lower over boiling water. Cover and steam for 2 hours. Lift out the lamb and allow to cool completely.

Just before serving, heat a pan of deep oil to 180°C/350°F. Deep-fry the pieces of lamb, in 2 batches if necessary, until browned and crisp.

Mix the ingredients for each dip separately and put into small bowls for serving.

MONGOLIAN BARBEQUED LAMB

900g/2 lb lean, boneless lamb, fillet or leg
bread rolls as required, at least 2 per person

SAUCE
2 tbsp black bean paste
2 tbsp soy sauce
1 tbsp Barbados sugar
1 tbsp sesame oil
1 tsp salt
½ tsp freshly ground black pepper
125ml/4 fl oz white wine vinegar
15g/½ oz fresh ginger root
½ green pepper
1 red chilli
4 spring onions
1 garlic clove

Cut the lamb into very thin slices. Divide between 4 small bowls. To make the sauce, put the bean paste into a bowl and gradually mix in the soy sauce, sugar, oil, salt and pepper. Stir in the vinegar

Peel and grate the ginger root. Core, seed and finely chop the pepper and chilli. Finely chop the spring onions and crush the garlic. Stir the ingredients into the sauce and divide between 4 small bowls. Cut the bread rolls almost in half crossways and remove some of the soft middles.

Lay a fine wire mesh or a metal plate over a barbeque grill. Oil lightly. Give each person a bowl of lamb and another of sauce. Using chopsticks or a fork, dip a small portion of lamb into the sauce and then lay it on the heated barbeque. Cook until done to your liking. Dip the lamb in the sauce again and place in the hollowed bread roll.

CHICKEN AND DUCK

Chickens and ducks are bred for the table in most parts of China. The most famous poultry dish of all is Peking duck which always takes pride of place at any meal in which it is served.

From Szechuan comes the tasty but easy to prepare smoked chicken and the light and flavoursome lemon chicken comes from the same area.

The Cantonese specialize in stir-frying chicken with vegetables, fruits and nuts. They also simmer chicken in a clear broth and set it in a crystal jelly.

CHICKEN WITH ALMONDS

2 chicken breasts
salt and freshly ground black pepper
150g/5 oz almonds
10 tinned water chestnuts
half 225-g/8-oz tin bamboo shoots
1 large onion
1 tbsp cornflour
2 tbsp soy sauce
200ml/7 fl oz chicken stock
3 tbsp oil
1 garlic clove, finely chopped
100g/4 oz bean sprouts

Skin the chicken and cut into 2cm/¾ in pieces. Season well. Blanch and skin the almonds. Thinly slice the water chestnuts and bamboo shoots. Thinly slice the onion. Put the cornflour into a bowl and mix in the soy sauce and chicken stock.

Heat the oil in a wok or large frying pan on a high heat. Put in the chicken pieces and stir-fry until they are brown and any moisture in the pan has evaporated. Remove. Put in the almonds and stir-fry until they are just beginning to change colour. Remove. Put in the onion and garlic and stir-fry for 1 minute.

Add the water chestnuts, bamboo shoots and bean sprouts and stir-fry for 2 minutes. Replace the chicken and almonds and stir to heat through. Stir the cornflour mixture and pour into the pan. Cook, stirring, until it has thickened to a translucent sauce.

PINEAPPLE CHICKEN

one 1.575-kg/3½-lb roasting chicken
4 slices fresh pineapple
1 red pepper
1 medium onion
1 tbsp cornflour
4 tbsp pineapple juice
2 tbsp soy sauce
1 tbsp white wine vinegar
150ml/¼ pint chicken stock
3 tbsp oil
1 garlic clove, finely chopped
1 tsp ground ginger

Bone the chicken and cut the meat into 2cm/¾ in dice. Core and dice the pineapple slices. Core and seed the pepper and cut into 2.5cm/1 in strips. Thinly slice the onion. Put the cornflour into a bowl and mix in the pineapple juice, soy sauce, vinegar and stock.

Heat the oil and garlic in a wok or large frying pan on a high heat. Put in the chicken and stir-fry until it browns and any moisture in the pan has been driven away. Add the pepper and onion. Scatter in the ginger. Lower the heat and stir-fry for 2 minutes. Mix in the pineapple. Stir the cornflour mixture and pour into the wok or pan. Stir until it thickens to a translucent sauce.

LEMON CHICKEN WITH PEPPERS

one 1.575-kg/3½-lb roasting chicken
salt and freshly ground black pepper
1 large onion
2 green peppers
thinly pared rind and juice of 2 lemons
1 tbsp cornflour
2 tbsp rice wine or dry sherry
2 tbsp soy sauce
175ml/6 fl oz chicken stock
3 tbsp oil
1 garlic clove, finely chopped
½ tsp ground ginger
¼ tsp chilli powder

Bone the chicken and cut the meat into 2cm/¾ in pieces. Season well. Thinly slice the onion. Core and seed the peppers and cut into 2.5cm/1 in strips. Cut the rinds of the lemons into thin slivers, blanch in boiling water for 2 minutes and drain. Put the cornflour into a bowl and mix in the lemon juice, wine or sherry, soy sauce and stock.

Heat the oil and garlic in a wok or large frying pan on a high heat. Put in the chicken and stir-fry until it browns. Put in the onion, peppers and lemon rinds. Lower the heat and scatter in the ginger and chilli powder. Stir-fry for 2 minutes. Stir the cornflour mixture and pour into the wok or pan. Stir until it thickens. Add the lemon rind and stir into the sauce. Reheat if necessary.

CHICKEN WITH CHILLI SAUCE

one 1.125-kg/2½-lb roasting chicken
1 tbsp cornflour
pinch of salt
1 egg white
12 tinned water chestnuts
15g/½ oz fresh ginger root
1 garlic clove, finely chopped
1 tsp chilli sauce
3 tbsp rice wine or dry sherry
2 tbsp tomato ketchup
2 tbsp malt vinegar
2 tbsp soy sauce
2 tsp Barbados sugar
oil for deep frying
2 tbsp sesame oil

Take all the chicken meat from the bones and cut into 2cm/¾ in pieces. Mix together the tablespoon of cornflour, the salt and egg white. Mix in the chicken. Halve the water chestnuts. Peel and grate the ginger. Mix the chestnuts and ginger with the garlic, chilli sauce, wine or sherry, ketchup, vinegar, soy sauce and sugar.

Heat a pan of deep oil to 180°C/350°F. Deep-fry the chicken pieces for about 2½ minutes or until they are golden brown. Drain on kitchen paper and keep warm.

Heat the sesame oil in a wok or large frying pan on a high heat. Mix in the sauce and bring to the boil. Add the chicken, stir to coat thoroughly and heat through for 1 minute.

CANTONESE CRYSTAL CHICKEN

one 1.575-kg/3½-lb roasting chicken
4 spring onions
15g/½ oz fresh ginger root
½ tsp salt
2 tbsp soy sauce
100g/4 oz lean cooked ham, thinly sliced
25g/1 oz gelatine
1 red pepper
1 green pepper

Truss the chicken and put into a saucepan or flame-proof casserole. Cut 2 of the spring onions into 5cm/2 in lengths. Peel and chop the ginger root. Add them to the chicken. Pour in cold water to just cover the chicken legs. Set the pan or casserole on a moderate heat and bring the water to the boil. Add the salt and soy sauce. Cover and simmer for 1 hour or until the chicken is tender. Lift out the chicken and cool completely. Strain and reserve the stock.

When the chicken is cool, cut into 24 pieces. Cut the ham slices into squares. Layer the chicken and ham in an oiled oval dish.

Soak the gelatine in 4 tbsp of the reserved stock. Heat the remaining stock to just below boiling point. Add the gelatine and stir until it dissolves. Remove the pan or casserole from the heat. When the stock is cold, pour it over the layered chicken and ham. Leave in a cool place for 3 hours for the jelly to set.

To serve, turn the jelly onto a flat serving plate. Garnish with strips of red and green pepper and the rest of the spring onion.

PEPPERED SMOKED CHICKEN

one 1.575-kg/3½-lb roasting chicken
2 tbsp Szechuan or black peppercorns
1 tbsp salt
3 tbsp dark brown sugar
2 tbsp Chinese tea leaves or pine needles
1 tsp ground ginger
2 tbsp sesame oil

Cook the peppercorns in a dry pan over a medium heat for 3 minutes. Crush coarsely, mix with the salt and rub into the chicken skin and inside the body cavity.

Place the chicken in a steamer over gently boiling water. Cover and steam for 1 hour. Lift out the chicken and allow to cool.

Line a large, heavy casserole with aluminium foil. Mix together the sugar, tea leaves or pine needles and ginger and put into the casserole. Place a wire rack inside and put the chicken on the rack. Bring the sides of the foil over the chicken and seal the foil. Put on the lid.

Set the casserole on a moderate heat for 15 minutes. Turn off the heat and leave the chicken standing for 5 minutes. Brush the chicken with the sesame oil before jointing and serving.

DEEP-FRIED PAPER-WRAPPED CHICKEN

one 1.5-kg/3-lb roasting chicken
3 tbsp rice wine or dry sherry
2 tbsp oil
3 tbsp soy sauce
¼ tsp salt
4 spring onions, finely chopped
15g/½ oz fresh ginger root, peeled and grated
22 pieces greaseproof paper 12.5cm/5 in square
oil for deep frying
cucumber, lettuce, radishes or watercress

Take all the chicken meat from the bones and cut into small, thin slivers. Mix the chicken slivers in a bowl with the wine or sherry, oil, soy sauce, salt, spring onions and ginger. Leave to marinate for 2 hours at room temperature.

To make the paper parcels, put about 1 tbsp of the chicken towards one corner of the piece of greaseproof paper. Fold over the nearest corner (1), the two sides (2, 3) and continue to fold from the opposite corner (4). Tuck in the final corner (5) to prevent the parcel from coming apart.

Heat a pan of deep oil to 180°C/350°F. Deep-fry the parcels, 4 or 5 at a time. Drain the parcels on a rack and keep warm while you fry the rest.

To serve, arrange the parcels in overlapping lines or circles on a warmed serving plate. Garnish with salad vegetables.

PEKING DUCK

one 1.8-kg/4-lb duck
3 tbsp honey
15g/½ oz fresh ginger root, peeled and
    chopped
2 spring onions, cut into 2.5cm/1 in lengths
2 tbsp Barbados sugar
2 tbsp rice wine or dry sherry
½ tsp salt

SAUCE
100ml/3½ fl oz hoisin sauce
2 tbsp soy sauce
1 tbsp sesame oil

FOR SERVING
Mandarin pancakes (p. 70)
1 cucumber
6 celery sticks
12 spring onions

Put enough boiling water to cover the duck in a
large saucepan or flameproof casserole. Add the
honey, ginger root and spring onions. Put in the
duck and turn it in the water. Leave for 1 minute.
Take out the duck and drain. Hang up in a cool,
airy place overnight to dry.

Two hours before cooking, mix together the
sugar, wine or sherry and salt. Brush the mixture
over the duck. Hang the duck up again to dry.

Heat the oven to 190°C/375°F/Gas 5. Place the
duck on a rack in a roasting tin and put into the
oven for 20 minutes. Turn the temperature to
150°C/300°/Gas 2 and continue cooking for 1 hour.
Raise the temperature to 200°C/400°F/Gas 6 and
cook for a further 20–30 minutes by which time the
duck should be tender and the skin very crisp.

While the duck is cooking, make the Mandarin
pancakes. Cut the cucumber and celery into
5cm/2in sticks. Cut half the spring onions into
7.5cm/3in lengths. Make several lengthways cuts
into each end and soak in iced water for 30 minutes.
The cut ends should curl to make what are often
called spring onion brushes. Finely chop the
remaining spring onions. Mix together the
ingredients for the sauce and put into a small bowl
for serving.

When the duck is cooked, carefully remove all
the crisp skin from the breast and front and cut into
5 × 7.5cm/2 × 3in pieces. Arrange the skin
separately on a serving plate. Remove the breast
and wings and slice the meat. Remove the legs and
cut each one in half. Arrange the meat and pieces of
leg on a serving plate.

Put the mandarin pancakes on a separate plate
and the cucumber, celery and spring onion brushes
on another. Each person takes a spring onion and
uses it to brush a little sauce over the pancake. A
piece of duck, skin, cucumber and celery and a few
pieces of chopped spring onion are placed on the
pancake which is then rolled and eaten with the
fingers.

SWEET AND SOUR DUCK

one 1.8-kg/4-lb duck
6 tbsp oil
1.8 litres/3 pints chicken stock
6 spring onions, cut into 2.5cm/1in lengths
15g/½ oz fresh ginger root, peeled and grated
4 tbsp soy sauce
2 egg whites
1 tbsp cornflour
2 green peppers
2 tbsp tomato purée
1 tbsp Barbados sugar
1 tbsp white wine vinegar
1 tbsp cornflour mixed with 3 tbsp water

Heat half the oil in a wok or large frying pan on a high heat. Put in the duck, brown all over and remove. Bring the stock to the boil in a large saucepan or flameproof casserole. Put in the duck, half the spring onions, all the ginger and 2 tbsp of the soy sauce. Cover and simmer for 1 hour. Lift out the duck and cool completely. Strain and reserve the stock.

Cut the duck into 5 × 2.5cm/2 × 1in slices. Beat together the egg whites and cornflour. Core and seed the peppers and cut into 2.5cm/1in squares. Mix together the remaining soy sauce, tomato purée, sugar, vinegar and 200ml/7 fl oz of the reserved stock.

Heat the remaining oil in a wok or frying pan on a high heat. In batches, dip the pieces of duck into the batter and fry until they are brown. Remove each batch and keep warm.

Put the peppers and remaining spring onions into the pan and stir-fry for 2 minutes. Pour in the sauce mixture and bring to the boil. Stir in the cornflour and stir until the sauce thickens. Return the duck to the pan and simmer for 1 minute to reheat.

EGGS

Eggs are used a great deal in Chinese cookery, both as the base for main dishes and also for coating meats and fish before they are stir-fried or deep-fried.

Thousand-year-old or hundred-year-old eggs have become legendary. They are in actual fact duck eggs that have been buried for 6–10 weeks in a limey clay that preserves and colours them.

The Chinese serve eggs in many different ways. Scrambled eggs are popular and can be mixed with seafood, lamb or beef. Plain boiled eggs are rarely served without being flavoured first either with soy sauce to give an effect rather like pickled eggs, or with China tea to give a light, delicate flavour.

Omelettes can be large and thick or very tiny. There are even fried eggs, a speciality of Szechuan, which are folded over to make them look like purses containing golden coins.

TEA EGGS

8 eggs
1 tsp salt
1 whole star anise (optional)
2 tbsp soy sauce
2 tsp China tea leaves

Hard boil the eggs for 10 minutes. Drain and tap the shells with a spoon to make a network of cracks all over the eggs.

Return the eggs to the saucepan and cover with fresh water. Add the salt, star anise, soy sauce and tea leaves. Bring the eggs back to the boil, cover and simmer for 1 hour. Cool them in the liquid for 2 hours.

Peel the eggs just before serving. They should be patterned with a brown marbling.

SOY EGGS

8 eggs
125ml/4 fl oz soy sauce
6 tbsp water
1 tsp Barbados sugar
¼ tsp salt
2 tbsp sesame oil

Boil the eggs for 5 minutes. Drain and pour cold water over them. Leave for 5 minutes, drain again and shell.

In a saucepan, mix together the remaining ingredients. Bring the mixture to simmering point and carefully put in the eggs. Leave on a very low simmer for 2 minutes, turning them halfway through. Take the pan from the heat and leave the eggs in the soy mixture for 3 hours, turning several times.

Cut the eggs into quarters. They can be served as an accompaniment or as part of a selection of hors d'oeuvres.

EGG POUCH OMELETTES

3 eggs
175g/6 oz minced beef
4 spring onions, finely chopped
1 tbsp soy sauce
¼ tsp ground ginger
½ tsp cornflour
salt and freshly ground black pepper
2 tbsp oil
2 tbsp chopped fresh coriander or parsley

SAUCE
1½ tsp cornflour
125ml/4 fl oz chicken stock
3 tbsp oyster sauce

Beat the eggs. Mix together the beef, spring onions, soy sauce, ginger, cornflour and salt and pepper.

Heat the oil in a frying pan or wok on a high heat. Put in 1 tbsp of the beaten egg and spread it out to make a tiny omelette. When the underside has set put a small portion of the beef mixture onto one side of the omelette. Fold over the other side and remove the omelette to a plate. Cook the rest in the same way. Put the omelettes into a steamer and set over boiling water. Cover and steam for 25 minutes.

Mix the cornflour with 2 tbsp of the stock. Bring the remaining stock to the boil in a saucepan. Stir in the oyster sauce and then the cornflour mixture. Stir until the sauce thickens and remove from the heat.

Put the cooked omelettes onto a warmed serving plate. Pour the sauce over the top and garnish with the coriander or parsley.

SCRAMBLED EGGS WITH PRAWNS

8 eggs
3 tbsp soy sauce
2 medium onions
4 tbsp oil
1 garlic clove, finely chopped
150g/5 oz bean sprouts
100g/4 oz shelled prawns

Beat the eggs with the soy sauce. Thinly slice the onions. Heat the oil in a wok or large frying pan on a high heat. Put in the onions, garlic and bean sprouts and stir-fry for 1 minute. Mix in the eggs and the prawns. Cook, stirring, until the eggs set to a scramble.

HAM AND VEGETABLE OMELETTES

225g/8 oz lean cooked ham
2 celery sticks
half 225-g/8-oz tin bamboo shoots, drained
1 medium onion
6 tbsp oil
100g/4 oz bean sprouts
2 tsp soy sauce
5 eggs
1 tbsp flour

Finely chop the ham and celery. Thinly slice the bamboo shoots. Finely chop the onion. Heat 2 tbsp oil in a frying pan or wok on a high heat. Put in the vegetables and stir-fry for 1 minute. Add the soy sauce, cook for 30 seconds and remove the pan from the heat. Turn the vegetables onto a plate to cool.

Beat the eggs and gradually beat in the flour. Mix in the ham and cooked vegetables.

Heat 2 tbsp of the remaining oil in the frying pan. Put in 2 tbsp of the mixture and cook until the underside is brown and the top is set. Turn over and brown the other side. Remove the omelette and keep warm. Cook the remaining mixture in the same way, using the last 2 tbsp of oil if necessary.

COIN PURSE EGGS

8 eggs
6 tbsp oil
salt and pepper
3 tbsp soy sauce
2 tbsp white wine vinegar
4 tbsp chopped fresh coriander or parsley

Heat 2 tbsp of the oil in a frying pan on a moderate heat. Break in 1 egg, if possible getting the yolk to one side. Season to taste. Fry until the underside is set. Fold over one side of the white to cover the yolk completely. Turn up the heat. Cook until the underside is brown. Turn the egg over and brown the other side. Transfer the egg to a warmed serving dish and keep warm. Cook the remaining eggs in the same way.

Mix together the soy sauce and wine vinegar and sprinkle over the eggs. Scatter the coriander or parsley over the top.

STEAMED PORK AND EGGS

225g/8 oz cooked pork
6 spring onions
6 tinned water chestnuts
¼ tsp salt
4 tbsp soy sauce
4 eggs
125ml/4 fl oz chicken stock
2 tbsp sesame oil

Finely chop the pork, spring onions and water chestnuts. Mix together and add the salt and half the soy sauce. Put the mixture into a heatproof serving bowl. Beat the eggs with the stock and pour over the pork.

Set the bowl in a steamer over boiling water. Cover and steam for 20 minutes or until the eggs are set. Mix the remaining soy sauce with the sesame oil and sprinkle over the top for serving.

CHICKEN FU YUNG

breast of 1 chicken
5 egg whites
2 tbsp rice wine or dry sherry
1 tsp cornflour
¼ tsp salt
4 tbsp oil
2 tbsp chopped parsley for serving

SAUCE
5 tbsp chicken stock
1 tbsp rice wine or dry sherry
¼ tsp salt
½ tsp cornflour mixed with 2 tbsp water

Mince the chicken. Mix with the egg whites, wine or sherry, cornflour and salt. Beat until smooth.

Heat the oil in a wok or large frying pan on a high heat. Pour in the chicken mixture. Cook until the mixture begins to look opaque. Stir to break it up. Keep stirring until the mixture sets, without allowing it to brown. Remove to a warmed serving plate.

Add the stock and wine or sherry to the pan and bring to the boil. Add the cornflour mixture and salt. Stir until the sauce thickens. Pour the sauce round the chicken. Garnish with the parsley before serving.

BEAN CURD

Bean curd is rather like a cheese that is made from soya beans. It comes in fresh, dried and fermented forms, but the recipes below all use the fresh variety. It looks like a thick white junket. It is usually sold in cakes of about 7.5cm/3 in square or in sealed cardboard packs.

Bean curd can be bought from Chinese shops and from many wholefood shops.

The taste of bean curd is rather bland and as a result it is often mixed with other foods in Chinese dishes. With plenty of vegetables and a tasty sauce, however, it can be made into a nutritious, high-protein vegetarian meal.

BEAN CURD WITH MUSHROOMS AND SPRING ONIONS

450g/1 lb bean curd
225g/8 oz mushrooms
10 spring onions
2 tbsp oil
2 tbsp soy sauce

Cut the bean curd into 6-mm/¼-in thick slices and the slices into 2.5cm/1 in squares. Thinly slice the mushrooms. Cut the spring onions into 2.5cm/1 in lengths.

Heat the oil in a wok or large frying pan on a high heat. Put in the mushrooms and spring onions and stir-fry for 1 minute. Add the bean curd and stir gently for 2 minutes trying not to break it up. Add the soy sauce and stir for 1 minute. Serve immediately.

FRIED BEAN CURD WITH OYSTER SAUCE

550g/1 lb 4 oz bean curd
2 spring onions
15g/½ oz fresh ginger root
2 tbsp rice wine or sherry
4 tbsp oil
1 garlic clove, chopped
3 tbsp oyster sauce

Cut the bean curd into 2cm/¾ in cubes. Cut the spring onions into 2.5cm/1 in lengths. Peel and grate the ginger root. Mix together the wine or sherry and stock.

Heat the oil in a wok or large frying pan on a high heat. Put in the ginger root, spring onions and garlic and stir-fry for 15 seconds. Put in the bean curd and stir-fry for 2 minutes. Add the wine or sherry. Stir for about 1 minute. Stir in the oyster sauce and remove the pan from the heat.

EGG-FRIED BEAN CURD WITH SHRIMPS

450g/1 lb bean curd
2 tbsp dried shrimps, soaked in warm water
  for 30 minutes and drained
1 leek or 4 spring onions
2 eggs
25g/1 oz flour
pinch of salt
50g/2 oz lard
300ml/½ pint chicken stock
1 tbsp soy sauce
2 tbsp rice wine or dry sherry
2 tbsp cornflour mixed with 2 tbsp cold water

Wrap the bean curd in muslin or in a clean linen tea cloth. Press gently to drain off any liquid. Cut the bean curd into 1-cm/½-in thick slices and each slice into 2.5cm/1 in squares. Finely chop the shrimps and the leek or spring onions. Beat together the eggs, flour and salt.

Melt half the lard in a wok or large frying pan on a high heat. Dip the pieces of bean curd in the egg batter. Fry the pieces until they are golden brown on each side, in several batches if necessary, adding more lard if needed. Remove the bean curd and clean the pan. Add the remaining lard.

Put in the shrimps and the leek or spring onions and stir-fry for 1 minute. Pour in the chicken stock and add the soy sauce and wine or sherry. Replace all the bean curd. Stir in the cornflour mixture and cook for about 2 minutes, stirring all the time, until the sauce thickens.

★ 100g/4 oz shelled prawns may be used instead of dried shrimps.

酒保强
換來藍裝
外門店酒間一坡漢在女少韓南名
鮮送餡陌機的機航民共中的

BEAN CURD WITH FISH IN CHILLI SAUCE

350g/12 oz bean curd
450g/1 lb firm white fish
3 tbsp soy sauce
3 spring onions
15g/½ oz fresh ginger root
4 tbsp oil
2 tbsp chilli sauce
2 tbsp rice wine or dry sherry
1 tbsp white wine vinegar

Cut the bean curd into 2.5cm/1 in cubes. Blanch in boiling water for 1 minute. Drain. Cut the fish into 2.5cm/1 in cubes. Sprinkle with 1 tbsp of the soy sauce and leave to marinate for 15 minutes. Finely chop the spring onions. Peel and grate the ginger root.

  Heat the oil in a wok or large frying pan on a high heat. Put in the pieces of fish to brown and remove. Put in the spring onions and ginger and stir-fry for 30 seconds. Stir in the chilli sauce, remaining soy sauce, wine or sherry and vinegar. Add the bean curd and simmer for 10 minutes.

BEAN CURD WITH HOT BEEF SAUCE

350g/12 oz bean curd
4 red chillis
3 tbsp oil
1 garlic clove, finely chopped
1 leek or 4 spring onions, finely chopped
100g/4 oz minced beef
2 tbsp soy sauce
2 tsp cornflour
100ml/3½ fl oz stock
1 tbsp sesame oil

BEAN CURD AND SESAME SALAD

350g/12 oz bean curd
½ medium cucumber
100g/4 oz cooked chicken
50g/2 oz roasted peanuts
oil for deep frying

DRESSING
2 tbsp sesame paste
1 tbsp soy sauce
1 tbsp white wine vinegar
1 tbsp rice wine or dry sherry
1 tsp chilli sauce
1 garlic clove, crushed with a pinch of salt
2 tbsp cold water

Cut the bean curd, cucumber and chicken into 1cm/½ in dice. Put the cucumber, chicken and peanuts into a bowl.

To make the dressing, put the sesame paste into a bowl and gradually work in the remaining ingredients to give the consistency of thick mayonnaise.

Heat a pan of deep oil to 180°C/350°F. Add the cubes of bean curd and deep fry until they are just turning brown. Remove and drain. Heat the oil to 190°C/375°F. Return the bean curd cubes to the pan and deep fry until crisp and golden. Drain quickly and mix into the ingredients in the bowl. Mix in the dressing.

Serve immediately – if the bean curd is left too long it will lose its crispness.

Put the bean curd into a saucepan of boiling water and cook for 1 minute. Drain. Cut into 1cm/½ in dice. Core, seed and finely chop the chillis.

Heat the oil in a wok or large frying pan on a high heat. Put in the garlic, leek or spring onions and chillis and stir-fry for 1 minute. Mix in the beef and stir-fry until it browns. Add the bean curd and soy sauce. Cover and cook gently for 10 minutes.

Mix the cornflour with the stock. Pour into the pan and stir for about 2 minutes. Take the pan from the heat and transfer everything to a serving dish. Sprinkle the sesame oil over the top before serving.

VEGETABLES

Many different kinds of vegetables are grown in China, both those familiar in the West and those that are not so well known. Chinese cabbage is used extensively and this has reached many temperate parts of the world in recent years. Other much used vegetables are red and green peppers, broccoli, spring greens, carrots and radishes. Onions, spring onions and leeks are added to nearly every dish as flavourers.

Vegetables in China are stir-fried, deep-fried and stir-braised, simmered in soy sauce, simmered in a clear broth and steamed. They are never eaten raw. Hot salads are made by stir-frying the vegetables first and then adding a vinegar-flavoured sauce. Salads to be eaten cold are made from blanched vegetables.

FRENCH BEANS WITH CASHEW NUTS

450g/1 lb French beans
150ml/¼ pint chicken stock
4 tbsp oil
75g/3 oz cashew nuts
1 garlic clove, finely chopped
2 shallots, thinly sliced
2 tbsp dry sherry
2 tbsp soy sauce

Top and tail the beans and break into 5cm/2in lengths. Bring the stock to the boil in a saucepan. Put in the beans, cover and simmer for 15 minutes or until just tender. Drain.

Heat the oil in a wok or large frying pan on a medium heat. Put in the cashew nuts and stir until they brown. Stir in the garlic, shallots and beans. Stir-fry for 1 minute.

Pour in the sherry and soy sauce and let them boil. Stir the beans to coat them and serve as soon as possible.

STIR-FRIED MANGE TOUT PEAS

450g/1 lb mange tout peas
4 tbsp oil
2 garlic cloves, peeled, left whole
4 tbsp dry sherry
2 tbsp soy sauce

Top and tail the peas. Heat the oil in a wok or large frying pan on a high heat. Put in the mange tout peas and garlic and stir-fry for 2 minutes. Remove the garlic. Pour in the sherry and soy sauce and lower the heat. Stir-fry for a further 2 minutes.

STIR-FRIED LETTUCE · WITH TWO SAUCES

2 Cos lettuces
2 tbsp oil
1 garlic clove, crushed
1 tbsp dry sherry
2 tbsp oyster sauce
2 tbsp soy sauce

Tear the lettuce leaves into 5cm/2in pieces. Heat the oil in a wok or large frying pan on a medium heat. Add the garlic and sherry. Put in the lettuce and stir-fry for 1 minute. Pour in the oyster and soy sauces. Let them boil and serve the lettuce immediately.

STIR-BRAISED MIXED VEGETABLES

25g/1 oz Chinese mushrooms
one 225-g/8-oz tin bamboo shoots
one 225-g/8-oz tin water chestnuts
150g/5 oz bean sprouts
1 medium onion
4 tbsp oil
1 garlic clove, finely chopped
100ml/3½ fl oz chicken stock
2 tbsp soy sauce
2 tbsp rice wine or dry sherry
2 tsp cornflour mixed with 2 tbsp cold water

Soak the mushrooms in boiling water for 20 minutes. Drain and halve them. Drain and thinly slice the bamboo shoots and water chestnuts. Thinly slice the onion.

Heat the oil and garlic in a wok or large frying pan on a high heat. Put in the mushrooms, bamboo shoots, water chestnuts, bean sprouts and onion and stir-fry for 2 minutes. Pour in the stock, soy sauce and wine or sherry and bring to the boil. Cover the pan and turn the heat to moderate. Cook the vegetables for 5 minutes. Add the cornflour mixture and stir until the liquid thickens to a clear sauce.

STIR-BRAISED VEGETABLES WITH ALMONDS

75g/3 oz almonds
1 small cauliflower
225g/8 oz carrots
1 green pepper
1 large onion
1 tbsp cornflour
2 tbsp soy sauce
300ml/½ pint chicken stock
4 tbsp oil
1 garlic clove, finely chopped
1 tsp ground ginger

Blanch the almonds. Cut the cauliflower into small florets. Thinly slice the carrots. Core and seed the pepper and cut into 2.5cm/1 in strips. Thinly slice the onion. Put the cornflour into a bowl and mix in the soy sauce and the stock.

Heat the oil and garlic in a wok or large frying pan on a high heat. Put in the almonds, cauliflower, carrots, pepper and onion. Sprinkle in the ginger and stir-fry for 2 minutes. Stir the cornflour mixture and pour into the pan. Bring to the boil, stirring. Cover the pan and cook the vegetables on a moderate heat for 10 minutes.

RED-COOKED CABBAGE

900g/2 lb green cabbage
1 medium onion
2 garlic cloves
15g/½ oz fresh ginger root
4 tbsp oil
4 tbsp soy sauce
2 tbsp rice wine or dry sherry
¼ tsp salt
½ tsp five-spice powder
1 tsp Barbados sugar
100ml/3½ fl oz chicken or vegetable stock

Cut the cabbage into 2.5-cm/1-in thick slices. Cut away the stem and cut each slice into quarters. Thinly slice the onion. Crush the garlic and peel and grate the ginger root.

Heat the oil in a saucepan or flameproof casserole on a high heat. Put in the cabbage and onion and turn them so they become well coated. Add all the remaining ingredients and turn the cabbage so they become well incorporated. Cover the pan and cook the cabbage on a low heat for 12 minutes.

HOT CELERY AND GREEN PEPPER SALAD

1 small head celery
2 green peppers
2 tbsp soy sauce
1 tsp chilli sauce
2 tbsp white wine vinegar
4 tbsp oil
1 garlic clove, finely chopped

Chop the celery. Core and seed the peppers and cut into 2.5cm/1in strips. Mix together the soy sauce, chilli sauce and vinegar.

Heat the oil and garlic in a wok or large frying pan on a high heat. When the garlic begins to sizzle, put in the celery and peppers. Stir-fry for 2 minutes. Add the flavouring ingredients and stir-fry for a further 1 minute. Remove the pan from the heat and serve immediately.

CARROT AND CHINESE CABBAGE SALAD

450g/1 lb carrots
1 tbsp salt
1 Chinese cabbage
4 tbsp sesame oil
2 tbsp soy sauce
1 tbsp white wine vinegar
½ tsp chilli sauce
1 garlic clove, crushed with a pinch of sea salt
2 tbsp chopped fresh coriander or parsley

Cut the carrots into matchstick pieces and blanch in boiling water for 2 minutes. Drain and put into a colander. Sprinkle in the salt and mix to coat the carrots. Leave the carrots to drain for 1 hour 30 minutes. Rinse through with cold water and drain again.

Cut the Chinese cabbage leaves into 5cm/2in pieces. Blanch in boiling water for 1 minute. Drain and arrange on a serving plate. Put the carrots in the centre of the bed of cabbage.

Beat together the remaining ingredients to make the dressing. Spoon the dressing over the carrots. Garnish with the coriander or parsley.

RICE

Rice is the staple food in most regions of China. Only Peking in the North uses more wheat than rice.

When you are serving rich dishes with a lot of sauce, a plainly cooked rice is the best accompaniment. To achieve a very light, fluffy effect, steam rice in the Chinese way, either in a bamboo steamer or a vegetable steamer.

Brown rice is not traditionally used in China but it can be used effectively for all the recipes below. You cannot steam it however, so use the boiling method for the basic cooking.

The rice dishes that contain extra ingredients such as prawns or diced meat can all be served to accompany lighter dishes and plainly cooked meats. Those with quite a large proportion of meat could quite well be served as a light snack meal, accompanied by soy sauce.

BOILED RICE

225g/8 oz long grain rice
600ml/1 pint cold water
pinch of salt

Put the rice, water and salt into a saucepan. Set on a moderate heat and bring to the boil. Stir, cover and simmer for 15 minutes or until all the water has been absorbed. Tip the rice into a colander or large sieve. Run through with cold water to stop the cooking process. Then run through with hot water to clear any stickiness.

Turn the rice onto a wide, flat dish and leave in a warm place for about 5 minutes to dry, fluffing it with a fork twice during that time to separate the grains and ensure even drying.

★ *To cook brown rice, increase the cooking time to 45 minutes.*

STEAMED RICE

225g/8 oz long grain white rice
salted water

Bring a large pan of salted water to the boil. Scatter in the rice, cover and cook on a low heat for 5 minutes. Drain, run through with hot water and drain again.

Put the rice into a bamboo steamer or a vegetable steamer. Set the steamer over boiling water, taking care that the water does not bubble up through the rice. Use the handle of a wooden spoon to make several holes through the rice for the steam to circulate.

Cover the pan and steam the rice for 45 minutes.

FRIED RICE WITH PEAS AND SHREDDED EGG

225g/8 oz long grain rice
2 eggs
3 tbsp oil
150g/5 oz cooked peas
2 tbsp soy sauce

Boil or steam the rice. Beat the eggs together. Heat 2 tbsp oil in a wok or large frying pan on a high heat. Pour in the eggs and cook until they are set.

Lift out the egg and cut into shreds. Put the remaining oil into the pan on a high heat. Put in the rice and peas and stir for about 1 minute until they are heated through. Mix in the soy sauce and half the egg. Put the rice into a serving dish and scatter the remaining egg over the top.

EGG–FRIED RICE WITH SPRING ONIONS

225g/8 oz long grain rice
10 spring onions
2 eggs
4 tbsp soy sauce
4 tbsp oil

Boil or steam the rice and allow to cool completely. Cut the spring onions into 4cm/1½ in lengths. Beat the eggs with the soy sauce.

Heat the oil in a wok or large frying pan on a medium heat. Put in the spring onions and stir-fry for 30 seconds. Fork in the rice. Pour in the eggs and soy sauce. Stir with a fork for 2 minutes or until the rice is quite dry with a light coating of egg.

EGG-FRIED RICE WITH CRAB

225g/8 oz long grain rice
6 spring onions
2 eggs
2 tbsp soy sauce
1 tsp chilli sauce
4 tbsp oil
100g/4 oz crab meat

Boil or steam the rice. Cut the spring onions into 2.5cm/1 in lengths. Beat the eggs with the soy sauce and chilli sauce.

Heat the oil in a wok or large frying pan on a high heat. Put in the spring onions and stir-fry for 30 seconds. Add the crab meat and stir-fry for 1 minute. Mix in the rice. Pour in the egg mixture. Cook, stirring constantly, until the egg has set to make a fluffy coating round the rice grains.

EGG-FRIED RICE WITH PORK AND PINEAPPLE

225g/8 oz long grain rice
225g/8 oz pork, cut into small shreds
6 tbsp soy sauce
2 eggs
4 tbsp oil
1 large onion, finely chopped
2 green peppers, cored, seeded and diced
1 garlic clove, finely chopped
4 slices pineapple, diced

Boil or steam the rice and allow to cool completely. Mix the pork with 2 tbsp of the soy sauce and leave to marinate for 1 hour at room temperature. Beat the eggs with the remaining soy sauce.

Heat the oil in a wok or large frying pan on a high heat. Put in the pieces of pork and stir-fry for 1 minute. Put in the onion, peppers and garlic, lower the heat and continue to stir-fry for 2 minutes.

Fork in the rice. Pour in the egg mixture and continue stirring with a fork for 2 minutes or until the rice is quite dry with a light coating of egg. Mix in the pineapple. Heat through for 30 seconds and serve as soon as possible.

HAM AND PRAWN FRIED RICE

225g/8 oz long grain rice
2 eggs
2 tbsp soy sauce
100g/4 oz lean cooked ham
3 tbsp oil
1 medium onion, finely chopped
100g/4 oz shelled prawns
100g/4 oz cooked peas

Boil or steam the rice and allow to cool. Beat together the eggs and soy sauce. Finely chop the ham.

Heat the oil in a wok or frying pan on a high heat. Put in the onion and stir-fry for 1 minute. Add the ham and prawns and stir-fry for a further 1 minute. Mix in the rice and peas. Pour in the egg mixture. Cook, stirring, for 2–3 minutes or until the egg mixture has set and lightly coated the rice grains.

Serve as an accompaniment to plainly cooked meats or as a meal in itself.

NOODLES

There are 3 types of noodles used in Chinese cooking. Egg noodles are made from wheat flour and are used mainly in the northern region; rice-stick noodles which look like thin, white sticks; and the thin, light transparent noodles. Egg noodles are sold in many supermarkets and delicatessens. You can usually only buy rice-stick and transparent noodles in Chinese shops.

Egg noodles need to be plunged into boiling water and cooked for 5 minutes so they are just tender. Rice-stick noodles and transparent noodles need only be soaked in hot water before being added to fried dishes. They can also be added to soups without soaking. They will cook in the soup in about 2 minutes.

EGG NOODLES IN YELLOW BEAN AND CHILLI SAUCE

350g/12 oz egg noodles
3 tbsp yellow bean paste
2 tsp chilli sauce
1 garlic clove, crushed
2 green peppers
1 medium onion
3 tbsp oil
150g/5 oz bean sprouts

Cook the noodles in boiling salted water for 5 minutes. Drain. Mix together the yellow bean paste, chilli sauce and garlic. Core and seed the peppers. Thinly slice the onion.

Heat the oil in a wok or large frying pan on a high heat. Put in the peppers, onion and bean sprouts and stir-fry for 2 minutes.

Add the noodles and stir in the sauce mixture. Heat through and transfer to a warmed serving dish.

PRAWN NOODLES WITH SESAME SAUCE

350g/12 oz egg noodles
1 tsp cornflour
1 egg white
175g/6 oz shelled prawns
6 spring onions
3 tbsp oil
2 tbsp soy sauce
2 tbsp dry sherry

SAUCE
3 tbsp sesame paste
6 tbsp water
2 tbsp soy sauce
2 tbsp red wine vinegar
1 tsp chilli sauce
1 tbsp sesame oil
1 garlic clove, crushed with a pinch of salt
4 spring onions, finely chopped

Cook the noodles in lightly salted boiling water for 5 minutes. Drain well.

Beat together the cornflour and egg white so you have a white froth. Mix in the prawns. Cut the spring onions into 2.5cm/1in lengths.

To make the sauce, put the sesame paste into a bowl and gradually mix in the water. Stir in the remaining ingredients.

To cook, heat the oil in a large frying pan or wok on a high heat. Put in the prawns and spring onions and stir-fry for 1 minute. Add the noodles, soy sauce and sherry and mix well. Cook, stirring, for a further 2 minutes.

Divide the noodles between 4 plates or bowls. Spoon the sesame sauce over the top.

CRISPY NOODLES WITH MIXED VEGETABLES

50g/2 oz Chinese mushrooms
225g/8 oz Chinese cabbage
one 225-g/8-oz tin bamboo shoots
half 225-g/8-oz tin water chestnuts
1 medium onion
1 tsp cornflour
2 tbsp soy sauce
225g/8 oz egg noodles
4 tbsp oil
oil for deep frying

Soak the Chinese mushrooms in boiling water for 30 minutes. Drain, reserving the water, and cut into quarters. Shred the cabbage. Thinly slice the bamboo shoots and water chestnuts. Thinly slice the onion. Mix the cornflour with the soy sauce and 4 tbsp of the reserved mushroom liquid.

Cook the noodles in lightly salted boiling water for 5 minutes. Drain and divide into 4 portions. Heat the 4 tbsp oil in a wok or large frying pan on a high heat. Put in the onion and stir-fry for 1 minute. Add the Chinese cabbage, bamboo shoots, water chestnuts and mushrooms and stir-fry for a further 2 minutes. Pour in the cornflour mixture and stir until it boils and thickens. Remove the pan from the heat, put the vegetables into a serving dish and keep warm.

Heat a pan of deep oil to 180°C/350°F. Put in one portion of the noodles, keeping them together in an even round shape as far as possible. Deep-fry for about 6 minutes until they are crisp and brown, turning once. Lift out the noodles and drain on kitchen paper. Reheat the oil and cook the remaining noodles in the same way.

To serve, put the portions of crispy noodles on top of the vegetables.

EGG NOODLES WITH PORK AND MIXED VEGETABLES

100g/4 oz lean pork
1 tbsp cornflour
1 tbsp soy sauce
1 tbsp rice wine or dry sherry
350g/12 oz egg noodles
100g/4 oz Chinese cabbage
100g/4 oz mushrooms
1 green pepper
1 medium onion
4 tbsp oil

Cut the pork into 6mm × 2.5cm/¼ × 1in pieces. Mix together the cornflour, soy sauce and wine or sherry. Stir in the pork. Cook the egg noodles in lightly salted boiling water for 5 minutes. Drain.

Finely shred the cabbage. Thinly slice the mushrooms. Cut the pepper into 2.5cm/1in strips. Thinly slice the onion.

Heat the oil in a large frying pan or wok on a high heat. Put in the pork and stir-fry until it browns. Add the vegetables, lower the heat and stir-fry for 2 minutes. Mix in the noodles and stir on the heat for 2 minutes to heat through.

This dish can be served as a light meal or as an accompaniment.

RICE-STICK NOODLES WITH SHRIMPS AND HAM

350g/12 oz rice-stick noodles
25g/1 oz dried shrimps
75g/3 oz lean cooked ham
3 celery sticks
1 small onion
half 225-g/8-oz tin bamboo shoots
4 tbsp oil
2 tbsp soy sauce
2 tbsp stock

Soak the noodles in warm water for about 15 minutes until they are soft. Drain. Soak the dried shrimps in warm water for 45 minutes and drain. Cut the ham and celery into small, thin shreds. Thinly slice the onion and the bamboo shoots.

Heat half the oil in a wok or large frying pan on a high heat. Put in the onion, celery, bamboo shoots and shrimps and stir-fry for 2 minutes. Add the ham and stir-fry for a further 1 minute. Remove the contents of the pan and keep warm. Put in the remaining oil and add the noodles. Stir-fry for 2 minutes. Add the prawn and ham mixture, the soy sauce and the stock. Stir for 2 minutes or until all the liquid has evaporated.

TRANSPARENT NOODLES WITH PORK

100g/4 oz transparent noodles
225g/8 oz lean pork
1 tsp cornflour
2 tbsp soy sauce
4 spring onions
1 green chilli
1 tbsp hot black bean paste
125ml/4 fl oz chicken stock or water
4 tbsp oil

Soak the noodles in warm water for 10 minutes. Drain. Finely mince the pork and mix with the cornflour and soy sauce. Finely chop the spring onions. Core, seed and finely chop the chilli. Mix the bean paste with the stock or water.

Heat the oil in a wok or large frying pan on a high heat. Put in the pork and stir-fry for about 2 minutes until it browns. Stir in the noodles, spring onions, chilli and then the bean paste mixture. Bring to the boil and stir for about 1 minute until all the moisture has evaporated.

PANCAKES, ROLLS AND DIM SUM DISHES

In the northern area of China where wheat is the staple food, plain pancakes are often made to accompany the meal. The most famous of these are the Mandarin pancakes which are used to accompany duck dishes – in particular Peking duck.

A speciality of Canton is the dim sum meal. Dim sum means 'to please the heart' and essentially the meal is a pleasant snack, eaten in the middle of the morning or the afternoon, usually at a local restaurant.

Steamed buns both sweet and savoury, deep-fried or steamed wantons and spring and egg rolls can all feature in a dim sum meal.

MANDARIN PANCAKES

450g/1 lb flour
300ml/½ pint boiling water
1 tbsp oil
3 tbsp sesame oil

Sift the flour into a mixing bowl and make a well in the centre. Mix together the water and oil and gradually stir into the flour using chopsticks or a wooden spoon. Turn the dough onto a floured work top and knead until firm. Let the dough rest for 10 minutes.

Divide the dough into 3 and roll each piece into a sausage shape about 5cm/2in in diameter. Cut each one into 8. Roll the small pieces to thin, flat pancakes about 18cm/7in in diameter. Brush one side of half the pancakes with sesame oil. Sandwich them together with the remaining pancakes.

Set a heavy frying pan on a high heat without any fat. When the pan is hot, reduce the heat to moderate. Fry one pancake sandwich at a time, turning it over when it starts to rise and bubble and when small brown spots appear on the underside.

When both sides are done, gently peel the 2 pancakes apart and fold each one in half, oiled side inwards. Cook the remaining pancakes in the same way, keeping them warm in a low oven as the rest are cooked.

The pancakes can be made in advance, wrapped in a clean linen tea cloth and reheated in a low oven when needed.

PORK AND SPRING ONION PANCAKES

**pancake dough made as for Mandarin
  pancakes, half quantity**
100g/4 oz cooked pork
6 spring onions
1 tbsp salt
2 tbsp rice wine or dry sherry
1 tbsp sesame oil
oil for shallow frying

Cut the dough into pieces as for Mandarin pancakes. Roll each piece into a long, flat oval shape.

Finely chop the pork and spring onions. Mix with the salt, wine or sherry and sesame oil. Scatter about 1 tbsp of the filling over each pancake. Fold in the 2 long sides of each pancake to the centre and then fold each pancake in half lengthways. Form into a round, flat coil and tuck in the end. Roll the coil flat.

Shallow-fry each pancake in 2 tbsp oil for about 5 minutes on a moderate heat until brown on both sides. Serve hot.

DOUGH FOR STEAMED BUNS

25g/1 oz fresh or 15g/½ oz dried yeast
2 tsp sugar
3 tbsp warm water
450g/1 lb flour, plus extra for kneading
300ml/½ pint milk, warmed

If using fresh yeast, cream with the sugar and water; if dried, dissolve the sugar in the warm water and sprinkle in the yeast. Leave the yeast in a warm place for about 5 minutes or until it begins to froth.

Sift the flour into a mixing bowl. Make a well in the centre. Pour in the yeast mixture and the milk. Mix everything to a dough. Turn onto a floured work surface and knead until smooth. Return the dough to the bowl. Put the bowl into a greased polythene bag or cover with oiled cling-film.

Leave in a warm place for 1 hour or until the dough has doubled in size. Knock down the dough with your fist, cover again and leave once more for about 30 minutes until it has doubled in size. Knead the dough again until it is smooth and elastic.

★ *The quantities given here make about 24 steamed buns.*

STEAMED DATE AND NUT BUNS

dough for steamed buns, half quantity
50g/2 oz stoned dates (preferably Chinese red dates)
25g/1 oz shelled walnuts
25g/1 oz shelled almonds
1 tbsp sesame seeds
2 tsp lard, melted

Mince together the dates, walnuts and almonds. Mix in the sesame seeds and lard.

Form the dough into a sausage shape and cut into 12 pieces. Roll each piece into a 10cm/4in round. Put about 2 tbsp of the filling in the centre of each round. Loosely gather up the sides of the dough so they meet at the top. Twist round to secure the edges. Put the buns onto a sheet of floured greaseproof paper, cover with a clean tea cloth and leave to rise for 30 minutes.

Carefully put the buns into a steamer, leaving a 2.5cm/1in space between each one. Steam over boiling water for 10 minutes. If the buns have to be cooked in 2 batches, put those cooked first back into the steamer on top of those still cooking for the last 2 minutes of the cooking time.

WONTON WRAPPERS

450g/1 lb flour plus extra for rolling
1 tsp salt
2 eggs, beaten
200ml/7 fl oz cold water

Sift the flour and salt into a bowl. Make a well in the centre and pour in the eggs and water. Mix the ingredients with your fingers until you can make a soft ball. Knead the dough in the bowl until smooth.

Divide the dough into 4 and roll each piece to a thickness of 2mm/¹⁄₁₆ in. The dough can then be cut into squares or circles as needed. To cook, follow the method used for deep-fried pork wontons.

★ *The quantities given here make about 24 wonton wrappers.*

DEEP-FRIED PORK WONTONS

dough for wonton wrappers cut into 24
  7.5cm/3 in squares
150g/5 oz lean pork, minced
2 spring onions, finely chopped
4 tinned water chestnuts, finely chopped
½ tsp salt
2 tbsp soy sauce
oil for deep frying

Mix together the pork, spring onions, water chestnuts, salt and soy sauce. Place 1 tsp of the filling in the centre of each wonton wrapper. Moisten the edges of the wrapper with water. Bring one corner of the wrapper over the filling so it ends up just to one side of the opposite corner. Bring the other corners together under the folded edge, moisten with water and pinch together. As each wonton is finished, place in a plastic bag to keep it moist.

To cook, heat a pan of deep oil to 190°C/375°F. Drop in the wontons about 6 at a time and deep-fry for 2 minutes or until crisp and golden. Drain on kitchen paper.

SPRING ROLL WRAPPING

100g/4 oz flour
300ml/½ pint water
pinch of salt
oil for deep frying

Sift the flour into a bowl. Beat in the water to make a batter. Beat in the salt. Leave the batter to stand for 30 minutes.

Lightly grease a 20cm/8 in frying pan and set on a high heat. Spoon in 3 tbsp of the batter and spread it out quickly. Cook until the batter has set into a pancake. Remove and keep warm. Cook the remaining batter in the same way. This will make 8 pancakes.

To fill spring rolls, put 2 tbsp of the prepared filling onto the bottom half of each pancake. Fold over the bottom of the pancake to cover the filling. Fold in each side. Roll up the filling end to make a tight roll. Brush with a paste mixture of 1 tbsp flour and 1 tbsp water to seal the edge.

To cook spring rolls, heat a pan of deep oil to 180°C/350°F. Deep-fry the rolls, 2 at a time, for about 3 minutes until they are golden brown.

PORK AND VEGETABLE FILLING FOR SPRING ROLLS

225g/8 oz lean pork
100g/4 oz mushrooms
2 celery sticks
3 tbsp oil
1 garlic clove, finely chopped
100g/4 oz bean sprouts
3 tbsp soy sauce
2 tbsp rice wine or sherry
2 tsp cornflour

Thinly shred the pork. Thinly slice the mushrooms and finely chop the celery. Heat the oil in a wok or large frying pan on a high heat. Put in the pork and stir-fry for 2 minutes.

Stir in the garlic, mushrooms, celery and bean sprouts and stir-fry for 1 minute. Mix together the soy sauce, wine or sherry and flour and stir into the pan. Continue stirring until the mixture thickens. Remove the pan from the heat and let the filling cool.

WRAPPING FOR EGG ROLLS

75g/3 oz flour
300ml/½ pint water
6 eggs, beaten
oil for greasing and frying

Sift the flour into a bowl. Make a well in the centre. Gradually beat in first the water and then the eggs to make a smooth, thin batter.

Lightly grease an 18cm/7 in frying pan. Pour in 3 tbsp of the batter and spread it out quickly. Cook the pancake on one side only and remove. Cook the remaining batter in the same way.

To fill the pancake, put 2 tbsp of the prepared filling on the bottom of one pancake. Fold over the bottom of the pancake and then the 2 sides. Roll up the pancake and damp the edge with cold water to seal.

To cook egg rolls, heat a pan of deep oil to 180°C/350°F. Deep-fry the rolls 2 at a time, for about 10 minutes until golden brown. Drain on absorbent paper and keep warm in a low oven while you cook the rest.

PORK AND PRAWN FILLING FOR EGG ROLLS

100g/4 oz lean pork
100g/4 oz shelled prawns
75g/3 oz mushrooms
half 225-g/8-oz tin bamboo shoots
4 spring onions
3 tbsp oil
225g/8 oz bean sprouts
2 tbsp soy sauce
2 tbsp rice wine or dry sherry
1 tbsp cornflour

Finely shred the pork. Finely chop the prawns. Thinly slice the mushrooms and bamboo shoots. Finely chop the spring onions.

Heat the oil in a large frying pan or wok on a high heat. Put in the pork and stir-fry for 2 minutes. Add the prawns and stir-fry for 1 minute. Add the mushrooms, bamboo shoots, spring onions and bean sprouts and stir-fry for 2 minutes. Mix in the soy sauce, wine or sherry and the cornflour. Stir until the liquid boils and thickens. Remove the pan from the heat and cool the filling to room temperature.

SWEETS

Chinese sweets are many and varied, although many are rarely served in the West. Many are based on fresh fruits or fruits in syrup, making a refreshing end to a rich or salty meal. Almond cakes and deep-fried strips of sesame dough can be served with China tea. So too can the steamed sponge cake. This is very light and airy and traditionally eaten at the Chinese spring festival. The cubes of sweetened green pea purée are served as a sweetmeat to round off a late meal with friends.

WATERMELON BASKET

1 medium watermelon
1 small cantaloupe melon
2 oranges
3 peaches
one 225-g/8-oz tin lychees, drained
20 maraschino cherries
150ml/¼ pint sweet sherry
2 tbsp clear honey
150g/5 oz black grapes, in one bunch

Make a cut in the watermelon from the top end, down the centre to 2cm/½ in away from the middle. Make a similar cut from the base. Then cut round half the circumference of the melon from either end of the first cut. Remove the wedge of melon that is now cut away. Repeat on the other side so that you are left with a basket with a 2.5cm/1 in handle.

Scoop the pink flesh into balls using a Parisienne scoop (melon baller), discarding the seeds.

Cut the cantaloupe melon in half. Remove the seeds and scoop the flesh into balls. Cut the rind and pith from the oranges. Cut the segments away from the skin. Stone the peaches and cut them into thin, lengthways slices. Drain the lychees.

Put the prepared fruits into a large bowl. Add the maraschino cherries. Pour in the sherry and spoon in the honey. Chill for 30 minutes.

Put the melon basket onto a serving dish. Fill with the fruits. Hang the grapes from the handle.

ALMOND JELLY WITH FRUITS

100g/4oz almonds
450ml/¾ pint water
150ml/¼ pint evaporated milk
25g/1 oz caster sugar
25g/1 oz gelatine
¼ tsp almond essence
one 225-g/8-oz tin lychees in syrup
one 225-g/8-oz tin mandarin oranges in syrup

Put the almonds into a saucepan and cover with water. Bring to the boil. Drain the almonds and squeeze from their skins. Grind in a grinder, liquidizer or food processor.

Put the ground almonds into a saucepan with the 450ml/¾ pint water. Bring gently to the boil. Remove from the heat and leave for 30 minutes. Strain the almonds through fine muslin, squeezing to extract as much liquid as possible. Discard the almonds.

Put the liquid into a saucepan with the evaporated milk. Add the sugar and stir on a low heat to dissolve. Soak the gelatine in 4 tbsp water. Stir the gelatine into the almond mixture and let it dissolve. Add the almond essence.

Pour the jelly into a lightly oiled, shallow dish and leave in a cool place to set. Turn out and cut into diamond shapes.

Put the fruits and their syrups into a bowl. Put in the pieces of jelly and chill slightly before serving.

CARAMEL APPLES

4 crisp dessert apples
2 egg whites
2 tbsp cornflour
1 tbsp water
2 tbsp flour
oil for deep frying
225g/8 oz sugar
4 tbsp water
2 tbsp sesame seeds

Peel and core the apples. Cut each one into 8 lengthways slices. Mix together the egg whites, cornflour, water and 1 tbsp of the flour. Dust the apple slices lightly with the remaining flour and coat with the egg white batter.

Heat the oil to 180°C/350°F. Drop in 8 apple slices and cook until they are golden brown. Lift out and drain on kitchen paper. Cook the remaining apple slices in the same way.

To make the caramel, put the sugar into a saucepan with the water. Set on a low heat and stir until it dissolves. Bring to the boil and boil until it is light brown. Stir in first the sesame seeds and then the apple slices. Lift the apples onto a lightly oiled serving dish.

To serve, place a bowl of iced water on the table. Each person should take a piece of apple, either with chopsticks or a fork, and dip it into the water to harden the caramel.

STEAMED STUFFED PEARS

4 firm pears
50g/2 oz raisins
50g/2 oz walnuts
1 tsp ground ginger
2 tbsp honey

Cut 2.5cm/1in tops from the pears, leaving the stalks intact. Core the pears. Finely chop or mince the raisins and walnuts. Mix them with the spice and honey. Fill the pears with the mixture. Put the tops back on and anchor with toothpicks.

Put the pears upright on a heatproof dish and place in a steamer over gently boiling water.

Cover and steam for 30 minutes or until tender.

SWEET GREEN PEA CUBES

225g/8oz green split peas
600ml/1 pint water
75g/3 oz sugar
2 tbsp cornflour, mixed with 4 tbsp water

Soak the peas in the water for 4 hours. Bring to the boil, cover and simmer for about 45 minutes until they are soft. Put the peas and any remaining liquid through a fine sieve. Return to the cleaned pan.

Stir in the sugar and the cornflour mixture. Bring the peas to the boil, stirring. Turn the heat to the lowest setting and cook, stirring, for 10 minutes. Pour the mixture into a lightly oiled shallow dish or freezing tray so it is about 2.5cm/1 in deep. Chill in the refrigerator for 1 hour or until very firm.

Cut the peas into cubes and pile them up on a serving plate in a pyramid. To serve, spear the cubes from the plate using cocktail sticks.

DEEP-FRIED FRUIT BALLS

100g/4 oz stoned dates
75g/3 oz raisins
50g/2 oz whole dried apricots
50g/2 oz shelled walnuts
1 tbsp sesame seeds
2 egg whites
50g/1 oz cornflour
few drops red food colouring
oil for deep frying

Mince together the dates, raisins, apricots and walnuts. Mix in the sesame seeds. Form the mixture into about 20 small balls.

Beat together the egg whites, cornflour and food colouring. Heat the oil to 190°C/375°F. Dip the fruit balls into the batter and deep-fry them, 4 or 5 at a time, until they are crisp and golden. Drain on kitchen paper and serve hot.

SESAME SEED TWISTS

2 tbsp sesame seeds
225g/8 oz self-raising flour
15g/½ oz lard
50g/2 oz sugar
4 tbsp water
oil for deep frying

Put the sesame seeds into a heavy frying pan. Stir on a moderate heat until they brown. Tip out and cool.

Sift the flour into a mixing bowl. Rub in the lard and mix in the sugar and sesame seeds. Add the water and mix to make a soft dough.

Turn the dough onto a floured work top and knead lightly. Roll to a thickness of 3mm/⅛in and cut into 5×2.5cm/2×1in rectangles. Make a lengthways slit in the centre of each strip. Bring one end of the strip through to form a twist.

Heat a pan of deep oil to 160°C/325°F. Deep-fry the twists, 4 at a time, until golden brown. Drain on kitchen paper. Serve hot or cold.

ALMOND BISCUITS

175g/6 oz flour
pinch of salt
½ tsp bicarbonate of soda
75g/3 oz lard
25g/1 oz ground almonds
75g/3 oz sugar
1 egg
½ tsp almond essence
15 blanched almonds
1 egg yolk beaten with 1 tbsp water

Heat the oven to 180°C/350°F/Gas 4. Sift the flour with the salt and bicarbonate of soda. Rub in the lard. Mix in the ground almonds and sugar. Bind the mixture with the egg and essence and knead into a pliable dough.

Make the dough into 15 small balls. Lay on a floured baking sheet and flatten to a thickness of 6mm/¼ in. Press a blanched almond into the centre of each biscuit and brush with egg and water.

Bake the biscuits for 15 minutes or until they are light brown. Lift onto a wire rack to cool.

STEAMED SPONGE CAKE

6 eggs, separated
100g/4 oz caster sugar
3 tbsp water
100g/4 oz flour
½ tsp baking powder
1 tsp vanilla essence
1 tsp lemon essence
oil for greasing

Line a 20cm/8in cake tin with oiled greaseproof paper. Put a rack or trivet in a wok or large saucepan. Pour in water to just below it. Bring to the boil.

Whisk the egg yolks with the sugar and water until they are very light and fluffy. Sift in the flour and baking powder and beat until it is well blended in. Stir in the vanilla and lemon essence. Stiffly whip the egg whites and fold into the rest.

Pour the batter into the prepared tin. Put the tin into the wok or saucepan. Cover with a lid or greased foil and steam the cake for 30–40 minutes so it is firm and has shrunk slightly from the sides of the tin. Turn onto a wire rack to cool.

INDEX

Acknowledgements

We would like to thank: Valerie Clark, Jennifer Hudson, Sarah Goodman, Mitzie Wilson, David Schwarz, Chris Laing, Mr and Mrs V. Morris, Maggie Wire, Honesty Wholefoods, Union St., Maidstone, Kent, Boots Cookshops, Cheong Leen Supermarket, Tower St., London, WC2.